STEFAN WOLLE

UM BRUCH OST
LEBENSWELTEN IM WANDEL

TRANSFORMATION EAST
LIVES IN TRANSITION

Ⓜ | METROPOL

IMPRESSUM

Stefan Wolle

Umbruch Ost. Lebenswelten im Wandel. Begleitband zur gleichnamigen Ausstellung.

Transformation East. Lives in Transition. Companion volume to the eponymous exhibition.

Herausgegeben von der Bundesstiftung zur Aufarbeitung der SED-Diktatur und dem Beauftragten der Bundesregierung für die neuen Bundesländer.

Published by the Federal Foundation for the Study of the Communist Dictatorship in East Germany and the Federal Government Commissioner for the New Federal States.

ISBN: 978-3-86331-515-3
© 2020 Metropol Verlag
Ansbacher Str. 70
10777 Berlin
Germany
www.metropol-verlag.de
Alle Rechte vorbehalten.
All rights reserved.

Einbandgestaltung | *Cover design*:
Frank Kirchner, ultramarinrot, Berlin /
Thomas Klemm, Leipzig
Umschlagfoto | *Cover photo*:
dpa picture alliance / Jörg Carstensen
Satz | *Layout*:
Frank Kirchner, ultramarinrot, Berlin
Druck | *Printed by*:
buchdruckerei.de, Berlin

Die im Band abgedruckten Infografiken sind ein Beitrag von Statista zur Ausstellung „Umbruch Ost. Lebenswelten im Wandel". Weitere Zahlen und Fakten zur deutschen Einheit finden sich unter www.statista.de/ deutsche-einheit. Der Zugang zum gesamten Zahlenwerk ist an Schulen und Hochschulen entgeltfrei.

Die Ausstellung können Sie online bestellen unter: www.umbruch-ost.de

The infographics printed in this volume are a contribution from Statista to the exhibition "Transformation East. Lives in Transition". Further facts and figures about the reunification of Germany can be found at www.statista.de/ deutsche-einheit. Schools and universities can access all of this information free of charge.

You can order the exhibition online at www.umbruch-ost.de

INHALT / CONTENT

„Umbruch Ost. Lebenswelten im Wandel" ist der Begleitband zur gleichnamigen Ausstellung der Bundesstiftung zur Aufarbeitung der SED-Diktatur und des Beauftragten der Bundesregierung für die neuen Bundesländer. Das Buch präsentiert Texte des Berliner Historikers und Publizisten Stefan Wolle sowie 128 zeitgenössische Fotos renommierter Fotografinnen und Fotografen. Infografiken des Online-Portals Statista zur ökonomischen und gesellschaftlichen Entwicklung seit 1990 sowie Zeitzeugenvideos des NDR, die durch QR-Codes verfügbar gemacht werden, ergänzen den Band, der Schlaglichter auf den Alltag der deutschen Einheit – insbesondere in Ostdeutschland – wirft.

Die Ausstellung „Umbruch Ost. Lebenswelten im Wandel" kann als Poster-Set im Format DIN A1 gegen eine geringe Schutzgebühr für die schulische und außerschulische Bildungsarbeit bestellt werden. Darüber hinaus steht die Schau in weiteren Formaten und Sprachfassungen für die historisch-politische Bildung sowie die deutsche Kulturarbeit im Ausland zur Verfügung. Für weiterführende Informationen sowie didaktische Materialien zur Ausstellung besuchen Sie bitte die Webseite www.umbruch-ost.de

"Transformation East. Lives in Transition" is the companion volume to the eponymous exhibition produced by the Federal Foundation for the Study of the Communist Dictatorship in East Germany and the Federal Government's Commissioner for the New States. The book presents texts written by Berlin historian and publicist Stefan Wolle as well as 128 contemporary photos taken by renowned photographers. Supplemented by infographics examining the economic and societal developments since 1990, which were provided by the online portal Statista, and by contemporary witness videos (recorded by NDR and accessible via QR codes), the volume shines a spotlight on everyday life during reunification, especially in former East Germany.

The exhibition "Transformation East. Lives in Transition" can be ordered as a poster set in A1 format for a nominal fee for educational purposes and extra-curricular activities. The exhibition is also available in other formats and languages for the purpose of teaching history and politics, as well as for German cultural work abroad. For further information and educational materials relating to the exhibition please visit the website www.umbruch-ost.de

DER LETZTE TAG
THE FINAL DAY

Dienstag, 2. Oktober 1990. Am letzten Tag der DDR verhallen vor dem Berliner Reichstag die Lautsprecherproben für den feierlichen Staatsakt um Mitternacht. Als die Bier- und Bratwurstbuden öffnen, strömen die Menschen herbei. Ansonsten ist in der Stadt kaum etwas vom historischen Tag zu spüren. Im Westen ändert sich ohnehin wenig, und der Osten hat viele dramatische Umbrüche bereits hinter sich. Innerhalb eines Jahres sind dort Freiheit, Demokratie und deutsche Einheit erkämpft worden. Trotzdem ist die Stimmung eher nachdenklich. Was wird die Zukunft bringen? Alltagsprobleme haben sich in den Vordergrund geschoben. Im Grunde ist vielen klar, dass der Weg der wirtschaftlichen Angleichung steinig werden wird. Wer dies ausspricht, gilt rasch als Miesmacher. Wären doch die anstehenden Herausforderungen damals deutlicher ausgesprochen worden, mag man in der Rückschau denken. Die Freude über das Feuerwerk um Mitternacht wäre wohl nicht geringer gewesen, aber vielleicht die Enttäuschungen, die in den Jahren darauf folgten.

Tuesday, 2nd October 1990. On the final day of the GDR, loudspeaker tests in preparation for the formal act of state at midnight fade away in front of Berlin's Reichstag. As the beer and bratwurst stands open, people start to gather. Elsewhere in the city, there is virtually no indication of this historic day. There is little change in the West, and the East has already gone through several dramatic upheavals. In the space of a year, the East has won freedom, democracy and a unified Germany. Nevertheless, the atmosphere is somewhat pensive. What will the future bring? Everyday problems have been brought to the fore. It is ultimately clear to many that the path to economic alignment will be difficult. Anybody who expresses this sentiment is quickly branded a defeatist. In retrospect, one might think that the impending challenges could have been outlined more clearly at the time. The delight at the fireworks at midnight would likely not have been diminished, but the disappointment felt in the subsequent years perhaps could have been.

02-01 Letzte Wachablösung vor der Neuen Wache am Boulevard Unter den Linden, 2. Oktober 1990.
The last changing of the guard at the "Neue Wache" memorial on Unter den Linden, 2nd October 1990.

02-02 Zwei DDR-Grenzsoldaten am Grenzübergang Stolpe, 2. Oktober 1990.
Two GDR border guards at the Stolpe checkpoint, 2nd October 1990.

02-03 „Der Abend vor der Einheit" – letzte Vorbereitungen im Sendestudio des Zweiten Deutschen Fernsehens (ZDF) vor der Liveübertragung der Feierlichkeiten zur Wiedervereinigung.
"The evening before reunification" – final preparations in the broadcasting studio of Zweites Deutsches Fernsehen (ZDF, a public-service TV broadcaster) before the live transmission of the reunification celebrations.

02-04 Auf dem Opernplatz in Frankfurt am Main wird in der Nacht zum 3. Oktober 1990 gefeiert.
Celebrations on Opernplatz in Frankfurt am Main during the night of 3rd October 1990.

02-05 Auf der Tribüne vor dem Berliner Reichstagsgebäude ist in der Nacht vom 2. auf den 3. Oktober 1990 die politische Prominenz aus Ost- und Westdeutschland versammelt.
Prominent political figures from East and West Germany gather on the platform in front of the Reichstag in Berlin on the night of 2nd to 3rd October 1990.

02-06 „Deutschland, halt's Maul" lautet das Motto einer Demonstration gegen die deutsche Einheit am 3. Oktober 1990 in Berlin. Es kommt zu schweren Krawallen.
"Germany, keep your mouth shut" is the motto of a demonstration against German reunification on 3rd October 1990 in Berlin. It descends into serious rioting.

02-07 In der kleinen, südlich von Berlin gelegenen brandenburgischen Gemeinde Rangsdorf wird am 3. Oktober 1990 der „Thälmann-Platz" in „Platz der Deutschen Einheit" umbenannt.
In the small Brandenburg municipality of Rangsdorf, south of Berlin, Thälmann Platz is renamed "Platz der Deutschen Einheit" ("Reunification Square") on 3rd October 1990.

VIDEO
Die deutsche Einheit 1990,
zeitzeugen-portal.de, 3:38 Min.

The reunification of Germany 1990,
zeitzeugen-portal.de, 3:38 mins.

VIDEO
2019 haben sich zwölf Menschen für ein NDR-Projekt erstmals getroffen. Die einen wurden im Jahr des Mauerfalls geboren, die anderen 30 Jahre alt – Generationengespräche über die Deutsche Einheit, NDR 2019, 3:46 Min.

In 2019, twelve people met for the first time as part of a project run by Northern German Broadcasting (NDR). Some of them were born in the year that the Berlin Wall fell, others were 30 years old at the time; inter-generational discussions about the reunification, NDR 2019, 3:46 mins.

ENDLICH WESTEN
WESTERNERS AT LAST

„Das ist ja wie aus 'm Westen" – dieses Lob steht für die Messlatte, die die Ostdeutschen bis 1989 an DDR-Produkte anlegen. Die Warenwelt der Bundesrepublik kennt man aus dem Fernsehen, aus Geschenkpaketen und den Intershops, in denen sich Kaffee und Waschpulver zum Duft des Westens mischen und mit Westgeld zu bezahlen sind. Mit der Währungsunion am 1. Juli 1990 wird die ganze DDR über Nacht zum Intershop. Die heimischen Produkte verschwinden aus den Regalen. Niemand möchte mehr Milch von LPG-Kühen trinken oder Würstchen aus Halberstadt essen. Die Kunden wollen endlich die Herrlichkeiten kaufen, die sie so lange entbehrt haben. Als der Reiz des Neuen verblasst und Ostprodukte wie Spreewaldgurken oder Tempo-Linsen plötzlich wieder nachgefragt werden, sind viele ostdeutsche Hersteller längst pleite. Die wenigen DDR-Marken, die sich auf dem gesamtdeutschen Markt behaupten, sind inzwischen fast alle in westlicher Hand.

"That looks like it came from the West" – this praise is the yardstick which East Germans applied to GDR products until 1989. People recognised the array of products in West Germany (FRG) from the television, gift parcels and Intershops, in which coffee and laundry detergent recreated the smells of the West and were paid for with West German currency. The monetary union on 1st July 1990 turns the entire GDR into an Intershop overnight. East German products disappear from the shelves. Nobody wants to drink milk produced by the agricultural cooperative LPG any more, or eat sausages from Halberstadt. Customers want finally to buy the treasures that they have been deprived of for so long. As the allure of new things fades and East German products such as Spreewald gherkins and Tempo lentils are suddenly in demand again, many East German producers have long since gone bankrupt. The few GDR brands that hold their ground on the unified German market now have West German owners.

03-01 Vor dem Zirkus „Willkommen im Wunderland" kommt es zu einem Auffahrunfall zwischen einem Trabant und einem Opel, Halle (Saale) 1991.
An East German Trabant and a West German Opel collide in front of the „Willkommen im Wunderland" (Welcome to Wonderland) circus, Halle (Saale) 1991.

03-02 „Kommt die DM – bleiben wir. Kommt sie nicht, dann gehen wir zu ihr!" Die Sorge vor einer weiteren Massenabwanderung aus der DDR beschleunigt 1990 die Verhandlungen über eine Wirtschafts-, Währungs- und Sozialunion beider deutscher Staaten.
"If the Deutschmark comes to us – we stay. If not, we go to it!" Concerns of further mass emigration from the GDR accelerate the negotiations in 1990 over an economic, currency and social union of the two German states.

03-03 Eine Momentaufnahme in Cottbus 1990.
A snapshot in Cottbus, 1990.

kommt die-DM-bleiben wir
kommt sie nicht
dann gehen wir zu ihr!

03-04　In einem Supermarkt in Prenzlau (Brandenburg) studiert ein Kunde 1991 die Packung einer Tief-
kühlpizza.
In a supermarket in Prenzlau (Brandenburg), a customer examines the packaging of a frozen pizza in 1991.

03-05　Am 26. August 1991 eröffnet Möbel Höffner in Günthersdorf bei Leipzig die erste Niederlassung in
den neuen Bundesländern: Wie bei den Pkw auf dem Kundenparkplatz hält der Westen auch in den
Wohnungen rasch Einzug.
*On 26th August 1991, Möbel Höffner (a furniture retailer) opened its first branch in the new federal states
in Günthersdorf near Leipzig. Just like the cars in the customer car park, the West quickly finds its way into
people's apartments.*

03-06　„Aus unseren Bundesländern" wirbt ein Schild 1993 vor einer Kaufhalle in der Greifswalder Straße
in Berlin.
*"From our federal states" advertises a placard outside a department store on Greifswalder Straße in
Berlin in 1993.*

03-07　Die letzten Neuwagen der Marke Trabant warten in den 1990er Jahren auf Käufer.
The last newly built Trabant cars await buyers in the 1990s.

VIDEO
Thomas Krüger: Kosten der Einheit,
zeitzeugen-portal.de, 3:44 Min.

*Thomas Krüger: The costs of reunification,
zeitzeugen-portal.de, 3:44 mins.*

VIDEO

Westen – 1990 bedeutet für den Osten auch: neues Geld und … neue Autos. Die Währungsunion markiert unübersehbar einen Wandel im Alltagsleben, NDR 2019, 3:36 Min.

West Germany – For East Germans, 1990 brought new money and … new cars. The currency union marked an obvious change in everyday life, NDR 2019, 3:36 mins.

EINT
VOLK

VERTRAUEN
TRUST

„Helmut, nimm uns an die Hand und führe uns ins Wirtschaftswunderland" steht 1990 auf einem der Plakate, mit denen Bundeskanzler Helmut Kohl in Leipzig begrüßt wird. Noch im Jahr zuvor haben die Ostdeutschen ihrer eigenen Kraft vertraut und die SED-Diktatur entschlossen beseitigt. Nun richten sich ihre Hoffnungen auf den westdeutschen Bundeskanzler. Er hat nicht nur zur richtigen Zeit die richtigen Worte gefunden, sondern verkörpert mit Amt, Gestalt und pfälzischer Leutseligkeit den reichen Onkel aus dem Westen. In Sachsen werden Kurt Biedenkopf, in Thüringen Bernhard Vogel und in Brandenburg Manfred Stolpe zu Landesvätern, die – so die Hoffnung – es schon irgendwie richten werden. Doch als nicht alle Blütenträume reifen, wird aus Vertrauen Wut. Kohl und anderen Politikern schallen Pfeifkonzerte und Buhrufe entgegen. Wieder sind „die da oben" verantwortlich für alle Probleme, und es beginnt die Suche nach einem neuen Vater, der die Kinder an die Hand nimmt und ins vermeintliche Wunderland führt.

"Helmut, take us by the hand and lead us to the economic wonderland" is the message on one of the posters that welcomes Federal Chancellor Helmut Kohl to Leipzig in 1990. Just one year previously, East Germans had trusted in their own strength and deposed the SED dictatorship once and for all. Now their hopes are resting on the West German Chancellor. He not only found the right words at the right time, but with his office, stature and Palatine affability, was also the embodiment of the rich uncle from the West. Kurt Biedenkopf, Bernhard Vogel and Manfred Stolpe become father figures in Saxony, Thuringia and Brandenburg respectively, who – the hope is – will somehow straighten things out. But when these hopes are not fulfilled, trust turns to anger. Kohl and other politicians are met with barrages of whistling and booing. Once again it is "those at the top" who are responsible for all the problems, and the search begins for a new father figure who will take his children by the hand and lead them to the supposed wonderland.

04-01 Teilnehmer einer Wahlkampfveranstaltung in Cottbus mit Bundeskanzler Helmut Kohl am 15. März 1990, drei Tage vor der DDR-Volkskammerwahl.
Participants at an election rally in Cottbus with Federal Chancellor Helmut Kohl on 15th March 1990, three days before the GDR's legislative election.

04-02 Bundeskanzler Helmut Kohl bei einem Besuch in Erfurt im April 1991.
Federal Chancellor Helmut Kohl on a visit to Erfurt in April 1991.

04-03 Ein Arbeiter des Kalibergwerks Bischofferode im Hungerstreik, 1993. Das Transparent im Hintergrund appelliert an den Ministerpräsidenten Thüringens, Bernhard Vogel, die Schließung des Bergwerks abzuwenden.
A worker at the Bischofferode potash mine on hunger strike, 1993. The banner in the background appeals to the Minister President of Thuringia, Bernhard Vogel, to prevent the closure of the mine.

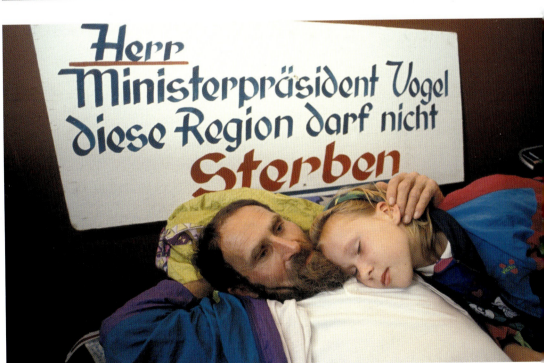

Kurt Biedenkopf.

Das Beste für Sachsen: **CDU**
DIE SÄCHSISCHE UNION

04-04 Der SPD-Kandidat in Berlin-Prenzlauer Berg Thomas Krüger wirbt bei der Bundestagswahl 1994 als „ehrliche Haut" um das Vertrauen der Wähler.
The SPD (Social Democratic Party) candidate in Berlin-Prenzlauer Berg, Thomas Krüger, campaigns for the Bundestag election in 1994 as an "honest soul" to gain the trust of the voters.

04-05 Die postkommunistische Partei PDS inszeniert sich in den 1990er Jahren erfolgreich als „Stimme des Ostens" und zieht immer mehr Protestwähler an. Ihr Zugpferd ist Gregor Gysi, hier bei einer Wahlkampfveranstaltung in Seelow (Brandenburg).
The PDS (Party of Democratic Socialism) successfully portrays itself in the 1990s as the "voice of the East" and attracts more and more protest voters. Its drawing card is Gregor Gysi, shown here at an election campaign event in Seelow (Brandenburg).

04-06 Beim Landtagswahlkampf in Sachsen wirbt Ministerpräsident Kurt Biedenkopf 1999 landesväterlich für die sächsische CDU, die fast 57 Prozent der Stimmen erzielt.
During the campaign for the state election in Saxony in 1999, Minister President Kurt Biedenkopf campaigns as a fatherly figure for the CDU (Christian Democratic Union), which receives almost 57% of the vote.

04-07 Bundeskanzler Gerhard Schröder bei seiner Sommerreise durch die neuen Bundesländer im August 2000. Für den Wahlsieg der SPD bei den Bundestagswahlen 1998 waren die Stimmen der Ostdeutschen entscheidend.
Federal Chancellor Gerhard Schröder on a summer tour of the new federal states in August 2000. The votes of former East Germans were crucial in the SPD's election victory in the federal election of 1998.

VIDEO
Helmut Kohl: Besuch in Dresden,
zeitzeugen-portal.de, 4:30 Min.

*Helmut Kohl visiting Dresden,
zeitzeugen-portal.de, 4:30 mins.*

VIDEO
Neuanfang – Ende 1989 jubeln Rostocker
dem sozialdemokratischen Altbundeskanzler
Willy Brandt zu. In der DDR jahrzehntelang
verordnete Gewissheiten schwinden,
NDR 2019, 3:15 Min.

*A new beginning – In late 1989, residents of
Rostock cheer the former Social Democratic
chancellor of West Germany, Willy Brandt.
In the GDR, decades-old certainties start to
disappear, NDR 2019, 3:15 mins.*

DEUTSCH-DEUTSCHE DEMOGRAFIE
THE DEMOGRAPHY OF GERMANY

Ökonomie / Economy

Arbeitslosenquoten in Ost und West nähern sich an
Unemployment rates in East and West are converging

Arbeitslosenquote (Ost / West)
Unemployment rate (East / West)

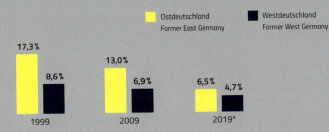

■ Ostdeutschland
Former East Germany

■ Westdeutschland
Former West Germany

17,3 %
8,6 %
1999

13,0 %
6,9 %
2009

6,5 %
4,7 %
2019*

* Durchschnittswert der Monate von Januar bis September | Average value for the months January–September

Arbeitslosenquote in Sachsen nur halb so hoch wie in Bremen
Arbeitslosenquote nach Bundesländern
(Stand: September 2019)

Unemployment rate in Saxony is less than half of the figure for Bremen
Unemployment rate by federal state
(as of September 2019)

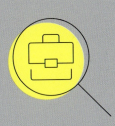

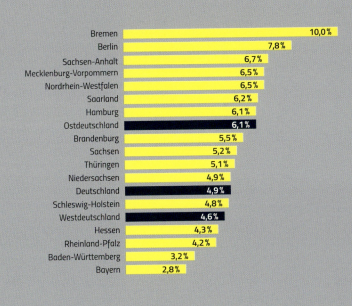

Bremen	10,0 %
Berlin	7,8 %
Sachsen-Anhalt	6,7 %
Mecklenburg-Vorpommern	6,5 %
Nordrhein-Westfalen	6,5 %
Saarland	6,2 %
Hamburg	6,1 %
Ostdeutschland	6,1 %
Brandenburg	5,5 %
Sachsen	5,2 %
Thüringen	5,1 %
Niedersachsen	4,9 %
Deutschland	4,9 %
Schleswig-Holstein	4,8 %
Westdeutschland	4,6 %
Hessen	4,3 %
Rheinland-Pfalz	4,2 %
Baden-Württemberg	3,2 %
Bayern	2,8 %

Kommunen in Mecklenburg-Vorpommern haben die geringsten Schulden
Verschuldung der Kommunen (Gemeinden/Gemeindeverbände) (in Mrd. Euro, 31.3.2019)*

Local authorities in Mecklenburg-Western Pomerania have the lowest levels of debt
Indebtedness of local authorities (municipalities/municipal associations) (in billions of euros, March 31, 2019)*

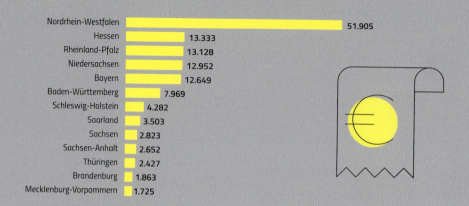

Nordrhein-Westfalen	51.905
Hessen	13.333
Rheinland-Pfalz	13.128
Niedersachsen	12.952
Bayern	12.649
Baden-Württemberg	7.969
Schleswig-Holstein	4.282
Saarland	3.503
Sachsen	2.823
Sachsen-Anhalt	2.652
Thüringen	2.427
Brandenburg	1.863
Mecklenburg-Vorpommern	1.725

* inkl. Wertpapierschulden, Kredite und Kassenkredite beim nicht-öffentlichen Bereich.
  incl. debt securities, loans and cash credit in the non-public sector.

Soziale Mindestsicherung ist in Stadtstaaten verbreiteter
Anteil Empfänger sozialer Mindestsicherung nach Bundesländern (2018)

Means-tested benefits are used more extensively in city states
Proportion of recipients of means-tested benefits by federal state (2018)

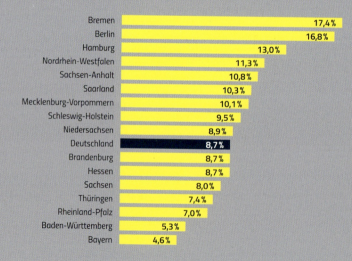

Bremen	17,4%
Berlin	16,8%
Hamburg	13,0%
Nordrhein-Westfalen	11,3%
Sachsen-Anhalt	10,8%
Saarland	10,3%
Mecklenburg-Vorpommern	10,1%
Schleswig-Holstein	9,5%
Niedersachsen	8,9%
Deutschland	8,7%
Brandenburg	8,7%
Hessen	8,7%
Sachsen	8,0%
Thüringen	7,4%
Rheinland-Pfalz	7,0%
Baden-Württemberg	5,3%
Bayern	4,6%

Ostfrauen sind beschäftigter
Beschäftigungsquote der Frauen liegt um ... Prozentpunkte über / unter der der Männer

More women in former East Germany are in employment
Female employment rate is... percentage points above / below the male rate

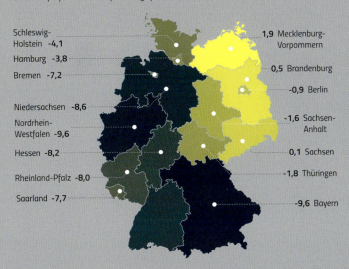

Schleswig-Holstein -4,1
Hamburg -3,8
Bremen -7,2
Niedersachsen -8,6
Nordrhein-Westfalen -9,6
Hessen -8,2
Rheinland-Pfalz -8,0
Saarland -7,7

1,9 Mecklenburg-Vorpommern
0,5 Brandenburg
-0,9 Berlin
-1,6 Sachsen-Anhalt
0,1 Sachsen
-1,8 Thüringen
-9,6 Bayern

Frauen in Führungspositionen
Frauenanteile unter West- und Ostdeutschen in führenden wirtschaftlichen Positionen (2019)

Women in leadership positions Proportion of women in former East and West Germany* in leading management positions (2019)

▮ Frauenanteile unter Ostdeutschen
Proportion of women in former East Germany

▮ Frauenanteile unter Westdeutschen
Proportion of women in former West Germany

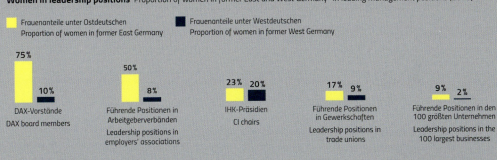

| 75% | 50% | 23% 20% | 17% 9% | 9% 2% |

DAX-Vorstände
DAX board members

Führende Positionen in Arbeitgeberverbänden
Leadership positions in employers' associations

IHK-Präsidien
CI chairs

Führende Positionen in Gewerkschaften
Leadership positions in trade unions

Führende Positionen in den 100 größten Unternehmen
Leadership positions in the 100 largest businesses

Ostdeutsche Frauen öfter in politischen Führungspositionen
Frauenanteile unter West- und Ostdeutschen in führenden politischen Positionen (2019)

More women in political leadership positions in former East Germany
Proportion of women in former East and West Germany in political leadership positions (2019)

▮ Frauenanteile unter Ostdeutschen
Proportion of women in former East Germany

▮ Frauenanteile unter Westdeutschen
Proportion of women in former West Germany

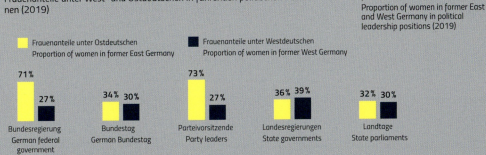

| 71% 27% | 34% 30% | 73% 27% | 36% 39% | 32% 30% |

Bundesregierung
German federal government

Bundestag
German Bundestag

Parteivorsitzende
Party leaders

Landesregierungen
State governments

Landtage
State parliaments

Demografie / Demography

Bevölkerungszahl im Osten stagniert
Anzahl der Einwohner in Ost- und Westdeutschland (in Mio.)

The population size in former East Germany is stagnating
Number of inhabitants in former East and West Germany (in millions)

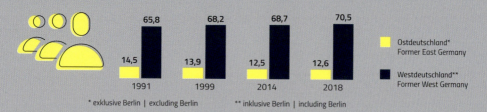

	1991	1999	2014	2018
Westdeutschland**	65,8	68,2	68,7	70,5
Ostdeutschland*	14,5	13,9	12,5	12,6

☐ Ostdeutschland*
Former East Germany

■ Westdeutschland**
Former West Germany

* exklusive Berlin | excluding Berlin   ** inklusive Berlin | including Berlin

---

Erstmals mehr Umzüge von West nach Ost als umgekehrt
Wanderungen zwischen West- und Ostdeutschland (in 1.000)*

For the first time, more people moved from West to East rather than the other way round
Migrations between Former East and West Germany (in 1000s)*

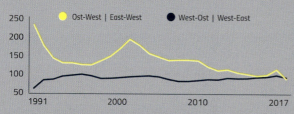

● Ost-West | East-West   ● West-Ost | West-East

* Ostdeutschland ohne Berlin | Former East Germany not including Berlin

---

Lebenserwartung in Ost und West gleicht sich an
Lebenserwartung bei der Geburt

Life expectancies in former East and West Germany are converging
Life expectancy at birth

■ Gesamt Overall   ☐ Ost Former East Germany   ■ West Former West Germany

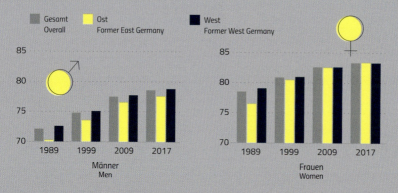

Männer
Men

Frauen
Women

Quellen: Bundesagentur für Arbeit, Bundesinstitut für Bevölkerungsforschung, RBB, Statistisches Bundesamt.
Sources: Federal Employment Agency, Federal Institute for Population Research, Berlin-Brandenburg Broadcasting, Federal Statistical Office.
Design: Cecilia Rojas, Anne Geick, Miriam Kaiser.

UM MU
BRUCH UM
OST 05

GEMEINSAMKEIT
COMMON GROUND

Selten ist der Plenarsaal des Bundestages in Bonn so gut gefüllt wie am 20. Juni 1991. Es geht um den künftigen Regierungssitz des vereinten Deutschlands. In den vierzig Jahren der Teilung haben Politiker aller Parteien stets betont, dass Berlin die Hauptstadt aller Deutschen sei. Doch als die Frage plötzlich konkret wird, wehrt sich nicht nur die Bonn-Lobby. Für viele Westdeutsche ist die Bundesstadt am Rhein ein Symbol für das demokratische, vom Großmachtstreben geheilte Nachkriegsdeutschland. Die von der Öffentlichkeit mit Leidenschaft geführte Debatte setzt sich im Deutschen Bundestag fort. Zwölf Stunden diskutieren die Abgeordneten. Am Ende gewinnt Berlin mit nur 18 Stimmen Mehrheit. Der Umzug von Regierung und Parlament wird erst 1999 beginnen. Zeitlich auf halbem Weg verwirklichen Christo und Jeanne-Claude im Juni 1995 ihre so lange geplante Reichstagsverhüllung. War der Berlin-Beschluss des Bundestages ein kritisierter, aber wichtiger Schritt für die innere Einheit, so versöhnt die Magie dieses Kunstprojektes die letzten Skeptiker mit der neuen Hauptstadt.

The assembly room of the Bundestag in Bonn has seldom been as full as it is on 20th June 1991. The matter under discussion is the future seat of government of reunified Germany. During the forty years of partition, politicians from all parties have consistently emphasised that Berlin is the capital of all Germans. But when the question suddenly needs answering, the Bonn lobby is not alone in making its case. For many West Germans, the federal city on the Rhine is a symbol of democratic post-war Germany, finally healed after a monumental effort. The passionate debate, which is led by the public, unfolds in the German Bundestag. Legislators discuss the matter for twelve hours. In the end, Berlin wins with a majority of a mere 18 votes. The relocation of the government and parliament will not begin until 1999. Midway through the 8-year wait, Christo and Jeanne-Claude realise their long-planned wrapping of the Reichstag in June 1995. As criticised as the Bundestag's capital decision is, it was taken in the interest of national unity and the magic of this art project reconciles the last few sceptics of the new capital.

05-01　Im Juni 1995 ist das Berliner Reichstagsgebäude für zwei Wochen verhüllt. Das Kunstprojekt von Christo und Jeanne-Claude entwickelt eine Ausstrahlung, die die Menschen weltweit in ihren Bann zieht.
In June 1995, the Reichstag building in Berlin is "wrapped" for two weeks. Christo and Jeanne-Claude's art project develops an aura that fascinates people around the world.

05-02　Die Bild-Zeitung jubelt am 21. Juni 1991 über den Beschluss des Deutschen Bundestags, seinen Sitz nach Berlin zu verlegen. Tatsächlich hatten sich 338 Abgeordnete für Berlin entschieden. Nach der langen Debatte war eine Berlin-Stimme zunächst übersehen worden.
On 21st June 1991, the Bild newspaper rejoices at the German Bundestag's decision to move its seat to Berlin. In fact, 338 legislators had voted in favour of Berlin. After a long debate, one vote favouring Berlin was initially overlooked.

05-03　Demonstration gegen den Regierungsumzug auf dem Bonner Münsterplatz am 20. Juni 1992, ein Jahr nach der Entscheidung des Deutschen Bundestages für Berlin.
A demonstration on Bonn's Münsterplatz against the relocation of the government, 20th June 1992, one year after the Bundestag's decision to move to Berlin.

05-04　Beim ersten Bundeswehrgelöbnis in Ostdeutschland leisten am 19. Oktober 1990 250 frühere
NVA-Soldaten in Bad Salzungen ihren Fahneneid.
*During the first oath ceremony in East Germany on 19th October 1990, 250 former soldiers of the
GDR take their oath of allegiance in Bad Salzungen.*

05-05　Einmarsch der deutschen Sportler bei den Olympischen Winterspielen 1992 in Albertville. Fahnen-
träger ist der Bobfahrer und frühere DDR-Spitzensportler Wolfgang Hoppe.
*Entry of German athletes at the Winter Olympics in Albertville in 1992. The flag bearer is bobsleigher
and former GDR elite athlete Wolfgang Hoppe.*

05-06　Bad Liebenwerda 1993: Auf ihren Bürgermeister Detlev Leißner lassen die Jugendlichen nichts kom-
men. Der Nordrhein-Westfale unterstützt ihre Forderung nach einem Jugend- und Kulturzentrum.
*Bad Liebenwerda 1993: These teenagers will not let anything happen to their mayor, Detlev Leißner.
The North-Rhine Westphalian supports their demand for a youth and arts centre.*

05-07　Fassadenkletterer arbeiten im Juni 1995 an der Verhüllung des Reichstagsgebäudes. Im Vordergrund
die Inschrift „Dem deutschen Volke".
*Industrial climbers work to wrap the Reichstag building in June 1995. In the foreground is the inscription
"Dem deutschen Volke" (To the German people).*

VIDEO
Bonn oder Berlin – die Hauptstadtfrage,
zeitzeugen-portal.de, 3:25 Min.

*Bonn or Berlin – the capital question,
zeitzeugen-portal.de, 3:25 mins.*

VIDEO

Gemeinsame Zukunft? – Für Berufssoldaten der NVA
1990 beinahe undenkbar. Aus zwei Armeen werden
nicht ohne Weiteres gemeinsame Streitkräfte des
vereinten Deutschlands, NDR 2019, 3:49 Min.

*A shared future? – Almost inconceivable for soldiers of
the East German National People's Army (NVA) in
1990. Merging two armies into one combined armed
force in the newly reunified Germany is not altogether
easy, NDR 2019, 3:49 mins.*

ERKUNDUNGEN
EXPLORATIONS

Den Menschen in der DDR ist eine Weltanschauung verordnet, doch die Welt anschauen dürfen sie nicht. Dabei würden sie sich nur zu gerne selbst vor Ort vom angeblich „verfaulenden Kapitalismus" überzeugen. 1990 ist es endlich so weit. Mit der neuen Zeit kommen die Verlockungen der großen, weiten Welt. Die Hochglanzbroschüren der neuen Reisebüros und die bunten Reklamen wirken seltsam fremd vor dem Einheitsgrau der ostdeutschen Städte. Sie versprechen traumhafte Paradiese, strahlend blaue Himmel, weiße Strände und ungeahnte kulinarische Genüsse. Und so ziehen die Ostdeutschen los, dies alles zu erkunden. Das Paradies finden sie nicht, aber der Himmel ist so blau und die Strände sind so weiß, wie sie es sich vor 1989 erträumt haben. Auch das Essen schmeckt besser als zu Hause. Bald sind die ostdeutschen Touristen nicht mehr von ihren Landsleuten aus dem Westen zu unterscheiden. In der Fremde sind sie im schlechten wie im guten Sinne einfach nur Deutsche. So wächst fern der Heimat oft schneller zusammen, was zusammengehört.

A particular world view is prescribed to the people of the GDR, and yet they are not permitted to view the world. Indeed, they would be only too happy to convince themselves of the vices of "festering capitalism" in the West itself. In 1990, that finally came to an end. Along with the new age come the temptations of the big wide world. The glossy brochures in the new travel agencies and the colourful advertisements appear almost alien against the uniform grey of East German towns. They promise dreamlike paradises, radiant blue skies, white beaches and unprecedented culinary delights. And so, former East Germans strike out to discover all of this. They do not find paradise, but the sky is as blue and the beaches as white as they had dreamed of before 1989. Even the food tastes better than what they have at home. Soon, East German tourists are hard to differentiate from their West German compatriots. Here on foreign land, they are, in both a good and a bad sense, simply Germans. Far from home, that which belongs together often grows together more quickly.

06-01 Das Reisebüro „ReiseWelt" in Chemnitz 1994. Die Familie entscheidet sich für einen Urlaub an der türkischen Riviera.
The Reisewelt travel agency in Chemnitz, 1994. The family decides on a holiday to the Turkish riviera.

06-02 Boarding in den neuen Airbus der DDR-Fluglinie Interflug am 3. April 1990 in Dresden. Das Ziel ist Mallorca.
Boarding the new Airbus owned by the GDR airline Interflug on 3rd April 1990 in Dresden. Its destination is Mallorca.

06-03 Weimar 1992: „Paradiesische Zustände" verspricht die Werbung jenen, die einen Platz für die Hawaii-Reise ergattern, die von der Zigarettenmarke gesponsert wird.
Weimar 1992: The advertisement promises "paradise-like conditions" for those who manage to grab a place on the Hawaii trip, which is sponsored by a cigarette brand.

36

06-04 Kulinarische Erkundungen auf heimischem Terrain: 1990 hat auf dem Ost-Berliner Alexanderplatz
       eine Döner-Kebab-Bude eröffnet.
       Culinary discoveries on home soil: in 1990, a Döner kebab stand opened on Alexanderplatz in former
       East Berlin.

06-05 Aus der Gaststätte „Aktivist" in Dresden ist 1994 das chinesische Restaurant „Mandarin" geworden.
       The "Aktivist" Gaststätte, or restaurant, in Dresden has become the "Mandarin" Chinese restaurant,
       1994.

06-06 Leipzig 1991: In der DDR war Pornografie verboten und das Angebot an Dessous hausbacken. So
       stoßen die ab 1990 überall in Ostdeutschland eröffneten Sexshops anfangs auf reges Interesse.
       Leipzig 1991: Pornography was banned in the GDR, and the selection of lingerie was plain. As a result, sex
       shops that opened in 1990 all over former East Germany were met with keen interest.

06-07 Unter dem Motto „Fremdsein erkunden" kommen im April 1994 Jugendliche aus Niedersachsen
       und Sachsen-Anhalt in Naumburg zusammen.
       Under the motto of "Fremdsein erkunden" ("Discover something different"), in April 1994 teenagers from
       Lower Saxony (in the former West) and Saxony-Anhalt (in the former East) meet up in Naumburg.

· ·

VIDEO
Rainer Ulbricht: Reisen nach dem Mauerfall,
zeitzeugen-portal.de, 1:32 Min.

Rainer Ulbricht: Travelling after the fall of the
Berlin Wall, zeitzeugen-portal.de, 1:32 mins.

· ·

VIDEO
Reisefreiheit – Was über Jahrzehnte in unerreichbarer
Ferne lag, ist plötzlich ganz nah. Die Ostdeutschen
machen sich auf, den Westen ihres Landes zu ent-
decken, NDR 2019, 3:00 Min.

*Freedom of travel – What was unreachable for decades is
suddenly close at hand. East Germans head off to discover
the West of their country, NDR 2019, 3:00 mins.*

UM UM
BRUCH
OST 07

AUFARBEITUNG
REAPPRAISAL

Im Lesesaal der Stasi-Unterlagen-Behörde ist Anfang der neunziger Jahre ein Mann in seine persönliche Akte vertieft. „Dieses Schwein", murmelt er vor sich hin. „Wie konnte er nur?" Offenbar ist er auf den Spitzelbericht eines Freundes oder Verwandten gestoßen. Dann packt er die Akten zusammen und verlässt mit Tränen in den Augen den Raum. Vielleicht hat er dem Verräter später eine in die Fresse gehauen. Vielleicht haben sie vernünftig über alles geredet. Wie auch immer die Geschichte ausgegangen ist, sie steht für einen Prozess, den die Gesellschaft durchlaufen muss. Die Abgründe des Verrats sind teilweise erschreckend. Doch nur durch die Öffnung der Akten ist es möglich, ein vollständiges und differenziertes Bild der Vergangenheit zu gewinnen und auch über persönliche Schuld und Verantwortung zu reden. Erst diese Aufarbeitung macht den Blick dafür frei, dass der DDR-Alltag eben nicht nur aus Stasi-Schnüffelei und Unterdrückung bestand.

In the early 1990s, a man is engrossed in reading his personal file in the Stasi Records Agency. "The bastard," he mumbles to himself. "How could he?" He has obviously stumbled across the informer report of a friend or relative. Then he packs up his files and leaves the room with tears in his eyes. Perhaps he later gave the betrayer a piece of his mind, or worse. Or maybe he talked everything over with them reasonably. However the story ended, it is symbolic of a process that all of East German society must go through too. The abysses of betrayal can sometimes be horrifying. But it is only by opening these files that it is possible to form a complete and nuanced image of the past and to talk frankly about personal guilt and responsibility. This reappraisal allows us to see clearly that everyday life in the GDR was not solely made up of Stasi snooping and repression.

07-01 Im November 1991 wird das Lenin-Denkmal vom heutigen Platz der Vereinten Nationen in Berlin-Friedrichshain demontiert.
In November 1991, the statue of Lenin on what is now Platz der Vereinten Nationen in Berlin-Friedrichshain is removed.

07-02 Transparente und Schilder, die bei der Großdemonstration am 4. November 1989 auf dem Ost-Berliner Alexanderplatz gezeigt wurden. Geschichtsbewusste Demonstranten sammelten sie nach der Kundgebung ein und übergaben sie später dem Museum für Deutsche Geschichte.
Banners and placards that were displayed at the huge demonstration on Alexanderplatz in East Berlin on 4th November 1989. Demonstrators with an awareness of history gathered them up after the demonstration and later gave them to the House of the History of the Federal Republic of Germany museum.

07-03 „Tut uns leid" – Graffiti am Marx-Engels-Denkmal 1991 im ehemaligen Ost-Berlin.
"Tut uns leid" ("We're sorry") – graffiti on the Marx-Engels Monument in former East Berlin in 1991.

07-04 Als im Januar 1992 die „Gauck-Behörde" ihre Arbeit aufnimmt, drängeln sich die Antragsteller in Frankfurt (Oder), um Einsicht in ihre Stasi-Akten zu nehmen.
When the Stasi Records Agency began its work in January 1992, applicants in Frankfurt an der Oder thronged to inspect their Stasi files.

07-05 Fort Zinna in Torgau (Sachsen) 1996: Ein Gedenkstein erinnert an die Opfer politischer Gewaltherrschaft. Zwischen 1936 und 1989 war die Anlage ein Ort der Repression – erst der Wehrmachtsjustiz, dann der sowjetischen Besatzungsmacht und schließlich der DDR.
Fort Zinna in Torgau (Saxony) 1996: A memorial stone commemorates the victims of political tyranny. Between 1936 and 1989, the facility was a place of repression – first by the Nazi military police, then by Soviet occupying forces and finally by the GDR.

07-06 Erich Mielke (links) und Erich Honecker (rechts), bis 1989 Minister für Staatssicherheit bzw. Staats- und Parteichef der DDR, auf der Anklagebank im Kriminalgericht Berlin-Moabit. Am 12. November 1992 beginnt der Prozess gegen die frühere DDR-Führung.
Erich Mielke (left) and Erich Honecker (right), Minister for State Security and Head of State of the GDR respectively, in the dock in Berlin's Moabit Criminal Court. The trial of the former GDR leaders begins on 12th November 1992.

07-07 Die spätere Bundeskanzlerin Angela Merkel und der CDU-Landeschef Klaus Preschle präsentieren im Landtagswahlkampf Mecklenburg-Vorpommern 1994 ein Plakat, das sich gegen eine mögliche Zusammenarbeit von SPD und PDS wendet.
Future Federal Chancellor Angela Merkel and CDU minister president in Mecklenburg-Western Pomerania present a placard in the state election campaign in 1994 appealing against a possible coalition between the SPD and the PDS.

VIDEO
DDR-Museum in Westdeutschland, DW TV, 3:33 Min.

GDR Museum in Former West Germany, DW TV, 3:33 mins.

VIDEO
Erinnerung – fällt nicht immer leicht. Ob ein Antrag auf Einsicht in die Stasi-Akten gestellt wird, bleibt stets eine sehr persönliche Entscheidung, NDR 2019, 5:45 Min.

Memories – Sometimes they can be difficult. Whether someone applies to view their Stasi files remains a very personal decision, NDR 2019, 5:45 mins.

AUFBRÜCHE
UPHEAVALS

Nach dem Mauerfall setzt eine große Wanderungsbewegung ein. Bis Ende 1990 verlassen rund 800.000 Menschen den Osten. Manche von ihnen waren zuvor vom SED-Grenzregime am Weggehen gehindert worden. Die meisten gehen, weil sie für sich in der Heimat keine Perspektive mehr sehen. Nach einem deutlichen Rückgang setzt um die Jahrtausendwende eine neue Abwanderungswelle ein. Im Jahr 2001 sind es fast 200.000 Menschen, die den Osten verlassen. Mit der Einwohnerzahl sinken die Steuereinnahmen und die Kaufkraft. Wohnungen stehen leer, Kindertagesstätten, Schulen und Kultureinrichtungen werden geschlossen. Ein Teufelskreis, der zu weiterer Abwanderung führt. Vor allem junge und leistungsorientierte Menschen gehen zum Studieren oder für eine Ausbildung in den Westen. Dort finden sie Jobs und oft auch Partner. Erst nach und nach kehrt sich der Trend um: Heute stehen den 3.681.649 Wegzügen der Jahre 1991 bis 2017 immerhin 2.451.176 Zuzüge gegenüber. Leipzig, Potsdam und das Berliner Umland weisen wieder positive Bilanzen auf. Noch sind die Folgen der großen Wanderung jedoch nicht überall überwunden.

The fall of the Berlin wall unleashes a huge wave of migration. 800,000 people leave the East by the end of 1990. Some of them had previously been prevented from leaving by the SED border regime. Most leave because they no longer see any prospects for themselves in their homeland. After a significant drop in numbers, a new wave of emigration sets in at the turn of the century. Some 200,000 people leave the former East in 2001. As the population decreases, tax revenues and purchasing power diminish too. Apartments are left empty, day care centres, schools and cultural institutions are closed. A vicious circle that leads to further emigration. It is young and ambitious people in particular who go to the West to study or train. They find jobs there and often a partner too. The trend only reverses very gradually: between 1991 and 2017, 3,681,649 people leave the East compared with 2,451,176 who move there. Things are looking more positive again for Leipzig, Potsdam and the area around Berlin. However, the impacts of this huge migration have not yet been overcome everywhere.

08-01 „Wir wandern aus!" heißt es 2007 in einem Ladenfenster in Grabow (Mecklenburg-Vorpommern).
"We're leaving!" exclaims a poster in a shop window in Grabow (Mecklenburg-Western Pomerania).

08-02 Quelle-Mitarbeiter aus dem thüringischen Suhl werden mitten in der Nacht zur Frühschicht nach Nürnberg gefahren. Foto: 1992.
Employees of Quelle (a furniture company) from the city of Suhl in Thuringia being driven through the night to Nuremberg for the morning shift. Photo: 1992.

08-03 Auf dem flachen Land schließen nach und nach – wie hier 2016 in Marzahna in Brandenburg – Geschäfte, Arztpraxen und Kneipen.
Shops, medical practices and pubs out in the countryside close one by one, like here in Marzahna in Brandenburg, 2016.

08-04 Ein Möbelwagen beim Auszug des letzten Mieters aus einem Plattenbau in Hoyerswerda-Neustadt (Sachsen) kurz vor dessen Abriss, Mai 2010.
A removals van transporting the possessions of the last tenant of a prefabricated high-rise in Hoyerswerda-Neustadt (Saxony) shortly before its demolition, May 2010.

08-05 Die Stadt Burg in Sachsen-Anhalt zählt 2014 rund 22.600 Einwohner. Seit der Wiedervereinigung sind 7.000 Bürger fortgezogen.
The town of Burg in Saxony-Anhalt has around 22,600 inhabitants in 2014. 7,000 residents have moved away since the reunification.

08-06 Hauptbahnhof Chemnitz: Passagiere steigen aus einem Sonder-ICE. Im Rahmen der Kampagne „Chemnitz zieht an" werden im Dezember 2018 potenzielle Rückkehrer aus Nürnberg abgeholt.
Chemnitz Central Railway Station: passengers disembark from a special ICE express train. As part of a campaign called "Chemnitz zieht an" ("Chemnitz is picking up"), in December 2018 potential returnees are fetched from Nuremberg.

08-07 Ein Schild mit der Aufschrift „Auf Wiedersehen" steht 2007 am Ende eines Dorfes nahe dem südbrandenburgischen Ortrand.
A sign with the message "Auf Wiedersehen" ("See you soon") is positioned at the end of a village near Ortrand in southern Brandenburg, 2007.

VIDEO
Rückkehr nach Ostdeutschland,
DW TV, 2:12 Min.

*Return to East Germany, DW TV
(Deutsche Welle is a state-funded but
independent broadcaster), 2:12 mins.*

VIDEO
Weggehen, bleiben, zurückkehren? – Seit 1990 haben sich viele Ostdeutsche diese Fragen gestellt. Oft waren es junge Menschen, die ihre Heimat verlassen haben, NDR 2019, 3:36 Min.

Move away, stay put or return? – Many former East Germans have asked themselves this since 1990. It was often younger people that chose to leave their homeland, NDR 2019, 3:36 mins.

UM UM
BRUCH
OST 09

ABWICKLUNG
WINDING-UP

Mehr als jede Statistik sagen die Gesichter der Menschen, die mit ihren Betrieben „abgewickelt" werden. Allein das Wort wird als zynisch empfunden. Für die westlichen Manager ist es ein Terminus technicus, für die Betroffenen der Verlust ihrer Biografie. In der DDR war Arbeit mit einem fast religiösen Nimbus umgeben. Natürlich war das auch politische Propaganda, gleichwohl stand im Alltag der Betrieb im Mittelpunkt des Lebens. Er sorgte für Kinderbetreuung sowie Sport- und Freizeitangebote, unterhielt Ferienheime, delegierte Mitarbeiter zum Studium und stellte sie später wieder ein. Zudem war im Betrieb für einige im ganz praktischen Sinne viel zu holen: ein Sack Zement, ein paar Bretter, eine Fuhre Sand. Und die Kollegen halfen sich gegenseitig, wenn es darauf ankam, etwas zu „organisieren". Das alles bricht 1990 weg. Dabei geht es nicht vorrangig um die verlorene materielle Absicherung, sondern vor allem um den Selbstwertverlust derjenigen, die sich bis dahin über ihre Arbeit definierten.

The faces of the people who are "wound up" along with their business say more than any statistic. Even the word – "Abwicklung" – is perceived as cynical. For Western managers it is simply a technical term, but for those affected in the East, it is the loss of their livelihood. In the GDR, work was surrounded by an almost religious aura. This was of course also political propaganda, and yet a person's business still formed the focal point of everyday life. It provided for childcare as well as sport and leisure activities, maintained holiday homes and afforded employees the chance to study with a job to return to later. Some people also took a lot out of a business in a practical sense: a sack of cement here, a few planks or a load of sand there. Colleagues helped each other out, when the need arose, to "organise" something. All of that disappeared in 1990. The loss that was most keenly felt was not that of material security, but of self-worth among those who had previously defined themselves through their work.

09-01 Besenreine Übergabe: 1991 übernimmt AEG das Transformatorenwerk Oberschöneweide.
Swept clean before the handover: in 1991, the electrical equipment giant AEG takes over the transformer factory Oberschöneweide.

09-02 1990 werden überall in der DDR Arbeitsämter gegründet. In Berlin-Marzahn informieren sich Ost-Berliner Bauarbeiter über Arbeitsmöglichkeiten im Westteil der Stadt.
Employment offices are set up all over the GDR in 1990. In Berlin-Marzahn, East Berlin construction workers find out about job opportunities in the western part of the city.

09-03 „Verkauft 1 DM" ist 1991 in einer Weimarer Fabrikanlage mit Kreide an eine Maschine geschrieben.
"Verkauft 1 DM", meaning "Sold for 1 Deutschmark" is written in chalk on a machine in a factory in Weimar, 1991.

54

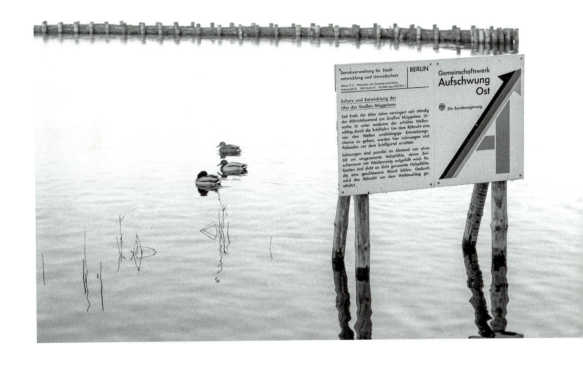

09-04 Arbeitsbeschaffungsmaßnahmen (kurz: ABM) und Umschulungen – wie hier 1991 in Bitterfeld (Sachsen-Anhalt) – gehören in den 1990er Jahren zum Alltag vieler Ostdeutscher.
Job creation measures (AMB) and retraining sessions – like this one in Bitterfeld (Saxony-Anhalt) in 1991 – were an everyday part of the lives of many East Germans in the 1990s.

09-05 Eine Artistin des Zirkus Berolina erreicht 1992 in Magdeburg die Nachricht vom drohenden Aus des früheren DDR-Staatszirkus.
In Magdeburg in 1992, a performer at the Berolina Circus receives news of the imminent closure of the former GDR State Circus.

09-06 Im Rahmen des Gemeinschaftswerks „Aufschwung Ost" werden u. a. Naturschutz-Maßnahmen am Müggelsee im Südosten Berlins finanziert. Foto: 1991.
Conservation measures at the Müggelsee Lake in south-east Berlin are financed as part of a collaboration called "Aufschwung Ost" (lit. "Upturn East"). Photo: 1991.

09-07 Die über 59.000 vietnamesischen Vertragsarbeiter, die bis 1989 in DDR-Fabriken beschäftigt waren, werden als Erste „abgewickelt". Ihr Bleiberecht war anfangs ungeklärt. Foto: Berlin-Marzahn, 1993.
The more than 59,000 Vietnamese contract labourers that were employed in GDR factories in 1989 are among the first to be "abgewickelt", meaning "wound up". At first, it was not clear if they had the right to remain. Photo: Berlin-Marzahn, 1993.

VIDEO
Wolfgang Nolte: Abbau West in Duderstadt,
zeitzeugen-portal.de, 3:35 Min.

Wolfgang Nolte: Losses to the West in Duderstadt,
zeitzeugen-portal.de, 3:35 mins.

VIDEO

Wie geht es weiter – wenn Betriebe verschwinden, Berufsabschlüsse nicht anerkannt werden, Arbeitslosigkeit droht? Das Ende der DDR ist für viele der Beginn sozialer Unsicherheit, NDR 2019, 6:00 Min.

What can anyone do when businesses are disappearing, qualifications are not recognised and unemployment looms? The end of the GDR is the beginning of social insecurity for many people, NDR 2019, 6:00 mins.

EINSTELLUNGEN IN OST & WEST
ATTITUDES IN THE EAST AND WEST

Selbsteinschätzung / Self-assessment

Ideale Lebensverhältnisse?
Zustimmung zur Aussage: In den meisten Bereichen entspricht mein Leben meinen Idealvorstellungen
Ideal living conditions?
Agreement with the statement: In most respects, my life corresponds to my ideal conception

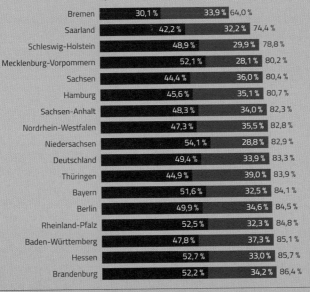

	Stimme (stark) zu / Agree strongly	Stimme teilweise zu / Agree to some extent	Gesamt
Bremen	30,1 %	33,9 %	64,0 %
Saarland	42,2 %	32,2 %	74,4 %
Schleswig-Holstein	48,9 %	29,9 %	78,8 %
Mecklenburg-Vorpommern	52,1 %	28,1 %	80,2 %
Sachsen	44,4 %	36,0 %	80,4 %
Hamburg	45,6 %	35,1 %	80,7 %
Sachsen-Anhalt	48,3 %	34,0 %	82,3 %
Nordrhein-Westfalen	47,3 %	35,5 %	82,8 %
Niedersachsen	54,1 %	28,8 %	82,9 %
Deutschland	49,4 %	33,9 %	83,3 %
Thüringen	44,9 %	39,0 %	83,9 %
Bayern	51,6 %	32,5 %	84,1 %
Berlin	49,9 %	34,6 %	84,5 %
Rheinland-Pfalz	52,5 %	32,3 %	84,8 %
Baden-Württemberg	47,8 %	37,3 %	85,1 %
Hessen	52,7 %	33,0 %	85,7 %
Brandenburg	52,2 %	34,2 %	86,4 %

Basis: 8.004 volljährige Erwerbstätige; April 2017
Base: 8,004 working adults; April 2017

West- und Ostdeutsche sind sich ähnlich
Anteil der Befragten, der verschiedenen Aussagen zum eigenen Leben zustimmt
Respondents from former East and West Germany produced similar results
Proportion of respondents who agreed with various statements about their own lives

West (inkl. West-Berlin) / West (incl. West Berlin)
Ost (inkl. Ost-Berlin) / East (incl. East Berlin)

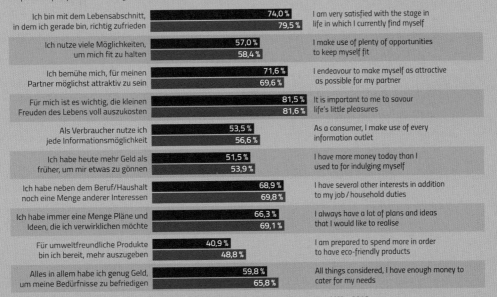

Aussage (DE)	West	Ost	Statement (EN)
Ich bin mit dem Lebensabschnitt, in dem ich gerade bin, richtig zufrieden	74,0 %	79,5 %	I am very satisfied with the stage in life in which I currently find myself
Ich nutze viele Möglichkeiten, um mich fit zu halten	57,0 %	58,4 %	I make use of plenty of opportunities to keep myself fit
Ich bemühe mich, für meinen Partner möglichst attraktiv zu sein	71,6 %	69,6 %	I endeavour to make myself as attractive as possible for my partner
Für mich ist es wichtig, die kleinen Freuden des Lebens voll auszukosten	81,5 %	81,6 %	It is important to me to savour life's little pleasures
Als Verbraucher nutze ich jede Informationsmöglichkeit	53,5 %	56,6 %	As a consumer, I make use of every information outlet
Ich habe heute mehr Geld als früher, um mir etwas zu gönnen	51,5 %	53,9 %	I have more money today than I used to for indulging myself
Ich habe neben dem Beruf/Haushalt noch eine Menge anderer Interessen	68,9 %	69,8 %	I have several other interests in addition to my job / household duties
Ich habe immer eine Menge Pläne und Ideen, die ich verwirklichen möchte	66,3 %	69,1 %	I always have a lot of plans and ideas that I would like to realise
Für umweltfreundliche Produkte bin ich bereit, mehr auszugeben	40,9 %	48,8 %	I am prepared to spend more in order to have eco-friendly products
Alles in allem habe ich genug Geld, um meine Bedürfnisse zu befriedigen	59,8 %	65,8 %	All things considered, I have enough money to cater for my needs

Basis: 23.086 Befragte (ab 14 Jahre) in Deutschland; 4 Befragungswellen zwischen Oktober 2016 und März 2018
Base: 23,086 respondents (aged 14 and over) in Germany; 4 survey waves between October 2016 and March 2018

Die Unterschiede zwischen Ost und West überwiegen
Überwiegen zwischen dem Westen und dem Osten Deutschlands eher die Unterschiede oder eher die Gemeinsamkeiten?

The differences between East and West outweigh the similarities
Is it the differences between former West and East Germany that dominate or the similarities?

■ Befragte in
Ostdeutschland
Respondents in
former East Germany

■ Befragte in
Westdeutschland
Respondents in
former West Germany

 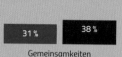

66 % 55 %

31 % 38 %

Unterschiede
Differences

Gemeinsamkeiten
Similarities

Basis: 1.297 Wahlberechtigte in Deutschland; Juni 2019 | Base: 1,297 eligible voters in Germany; June 2019

Trotzdem überwiegt die Zufriedenheit mit dem wiedervereinigten Deutschland
Wie zufrieden sind Sie alles in allem mit der Entwicklung in Deutschland nach der Vereinigung?

There is nevertheless widespread satisfaction with reunified Germany
How satisfied are you, all things considered, with the development in Germany since the reunification?

■ Sehr zufrieden /
überwiegend zufrieden
Very satisfied / mostly
unsatisfied

■ Überwiegend
unzufrieden /
sehr unzufrieden
Mostly unsatisfied /
very unsatisfied

65 % 34 % — September 1999
77 % 21 % — November 2014
79 % 19 % — November 2017
75 % 23 % — August 2019

Basis: jew. rund 1.000 Wahlberechtigte in Deutschland | Base: 1,000 eligible voters in Germany for each survey

Den Ostdeutschen geht es heute im Vergleich zu DDR-Zeiten besser
Anteil ehemaliger DDR-Bürger, der meint, dass es den Ostdeutschen im Vergleich
zur DDR heute besser / schlechter geht

East Germans are better off today than in the GDR era
Proportion of former GDR citizens who think East Germans are better / worse off today than in the GDR

65 % 14 % 13 %

Besser
Better

Schlechter
Worse

Kein Unterschied
No difference

Basis: 1.500 frühere DDR-Bürger, die heute immer noch in den fünf neuen Bundesländern leben und über 45 Jahre alt sind; August 2019
Base: 1,500 former GDR citizens who still live in one of the five former GDR states and are over 45 years old; August 2019

Ein Aufbruch der Bürger

Wird die historische Leistung der friedlichen Revolution im Herbst 1989 heute in der Öffentlichkeit gesehen als Leistung der ... (2009)

The citizens' awakening

The historic achievement of the peaceful revolution in autumn 1989 is still seen by today's public as an achievement of ... (2009)

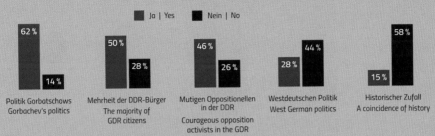

■ Ja | Yes   ■ Nein | No

| 62 % | 50 % | 46 % | 28 % | 58 % |
| 14 % | 28 % | 26 % | 44 % | 15 % |

Politik Gorbatschows
Gorbachev's politics

Mehrheit der DDR-Bürger
The majority of
GDR citizens

Mutigen Oppositionellen
in der DDR
Courageous opposition
activists in the GDR

Westdeutschen Politik
West German politics

Historischer Zufall
A coincidence of history

Basis: 1.920 Befragte (ab 18 Jahre); Juli 2009 | Base: 1,920 respondents (aged 18 and over); July 2009

Migration / Migration

Im Osten gibt es weniger Ausländer, aber mehr Vorbehalte
There are fewer foreign nationals in former East Germany, but more misgivings

○ Ausländeranteil*
  Proportion of foreign nationals*

● Befragte, die ungern ausländische Nachbarn haben**
  Respondents who do not like having foreign neighbours**

XX Fremdenfeindliche Übergriffe je 1 Mio. Einwohner, 2016 ***
XX xenophobic attacks per 1 million inhabitants, 2016***

Schleswig-Holstein 0,7
○ 7,7 % ● 22,0 %

Hamburg 1,1
○ 16,2 % ● 10,0 %

Bremen 0,0
○ 17,4 % ● 14,0 %

Niedersachsen 2,0
○ 9,0 % ● 21,0 %

Nordrhein-Westfalen 3,1
○ 12,8 % ● 20,0 %

Hessen 2,1
○ 15,7 % ● 17,0 %

Rheinland-Pfalz 1,2
○ 10,6 % ● 17,0 %

Saarland 5,0
○ 10,7 % ● 21,0 %

Baden-Württemberg 2,2
○ 15,1 % ● 18,0 %

9,3 Mecklenburg-Vorpommern
○ 4,3 % ● 31,0 %

6,8 Brandenburg
○ 4,4 % ● 31,0 %

2,0 Berlin
○ 17,6 % ● 19,0 %

11,2 Sachsen-Anhalt
○ 4,7 % ● 35,0 %

12,6 Sachsen
○ 4,6 % ● 43,0 %

7,4 Thüringen
○ 4,5 % ● 34,0 %

2,9 Bayern
○ 12,6 % ● 23,0 %

*   Stand: 30. November 2018 | As of: 30 November 2018

** Basis: 4.968 Befragte; 2017 | Base: 4,968 respondents; 2017

*** Angriffe auf Flüchtlinge, Brandanschläge auf Flüchtlingsunterkünfte, Demonstrationen mit justiziablen Vorfällen, Vandalismus
    Assaults on refugees, arson attacks on refugee accommodation, demonstrations with actionable incidents

Dreiviertel sind mit der deutschen Demokratie zufrieden
Befragte, die mit der Art und Weise, wie die Demokratie in Deutschland funktioniert,
alles in allem gesehen zufrieden sind

Three quarters are satisfied with German democracy
Respondents who are, all things considered, satisfied with the way in which democracy works in Germany

■ Sehr zufrieden | Very satisfied   ■ Ziemlich zufrieden | Fairly satisfied

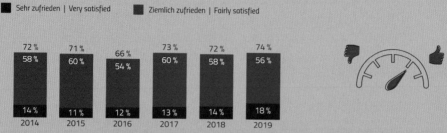

	2014	2015	2016	2017	2018	2019
Total	72 %	71 %	66 %	73 %	72 %	74 %
Ziemlich zufrieden	58 %	60 %	54 %	60 %	58 %	56 %
Sehr zufrieden	14 %	11 %	12 %	13 %	14 %	18 %

Basis: jew. rund 1.500 Befragte (ab 15 Jahre) in Deutschland | Base: approx. 1,500 respondents per survey (aged 15 and over) in Germany

Wovor haben die Deutschen Angst?
Befragte, die vor Folgendem große Angst haben

What are Germans concerned about?
Respondents who are particularly concerned about the following factors

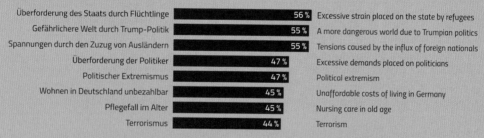

Überforderung des Staats durch Flüchtlinge	56 %	Excessive strain placed on the state by refugees
Gefährlichere Welt durch Trump-Politik	55 %	A more dangerous world due to Trumpian politics
Spannungen durch den Zuzug von Ausländern	55 %	Tensions caused by the influx of foreign nationals
Überforderung der Politiker	47 %	Excessive demands placed on politicians
Politischer Extremismus	47 %	Political extremism
Wohnen in Deutschland unbezahlbar	45 %	Unaffordable costs of living in Germany
Pflegefall im Alter	45 %	Nursing care in old age
Terrorismus	44 %	Terrorism

Basis: 2.400 Befragte (ab 14 Jahre) in Deutschland; Mai–Juli 2019 | Base: 2,400 respondents (aged 14 and over) in Germany; May—July 2019

Quellen: Amadeu Antonio Stiftung, ARD-DeutschlandTREND, Barmer, Bertelsmann Stiftung, Europäische Kommission, RTL / n-tv,
R+V Versicherung, Statistisches Bundesamt, Volkssolidarität, VuMA, ZDF Politbarometer.
Sources: Amadeu Antonio Foundation, ARD-Deutschlandtrend (an opinion survey of German voters run by ARD, an organisation
of public service broadcasters), Barmer, Bertelsmann Foundation, European Commission, RTL / n-tv (a German news channel),
R+V Versicherung, Federal Statistical Office, People's Solidarity, VuMA, ZDF Political Barometer (ZDF is a public-service TV broadcaster).
Design: Cecilia Rojas, Anne Geick, Miriam Kaiser.

Fällt der Name Treuhandanstalt, kochen bis heute die Emotionen hoch. Einig sind sich Kritiker und Verteidiger nur in einem Punkt: Die Treuhand stand bei ihrer Gründung am 1. März 1990 vor einer gigantischen Aufgabe. Ihr Auftrag war die Umwandlung der auf Staatseigentum basierenden Planwirtschaft in eine auf Privateigentum fußende Marktwirtschaft. Dafür war die Ausgangslage alles andere als günstig. Die Produktionstechnik der DDR war veraltet, ihre Produkte nicht marktfähig und der osteuropäische Absatzmarkt war zusammengebrochen. Hinzu kam der Schock der Währungsumstellung. Praktisch über Nacht waren die Gehälter 1:1 in D-Mark auszuzahlen. Dies brachte für die Betriebe eine ungeheure Belastung. Produkte, die zu Mauerzeiten in der DDR heiß begehrt waren und sogar in den Export gingen, wurden zu Ladenhütern. Was nun folgte, war in den Augen der Kritiker ein rücksichtsloser Kahlschlag. Für die Befürworter war es ein schmerzhafter, aber unvermeidbarer Weg der Sanierung.

Emotions run high to this day at the mention of the Treuhandanstalt (lit. "Trust Agency"). Its critics and advocates agree on just one point: the Treuhand was faced with a monumental task upon its founding on 1st March 1990. Its remit was to convert the planned economy with its focus on state-ownership into a market economy based on private ownership. The starting conditions for this assignment were far from favourable. The production technology in the GDR was outdated, its products were not marketable and the eastern European market had collapsed. Added to that was the shock of the currency conversion. Virtually overnight, salaries suddenly had to be paid at a ratio of 1:1 in West German Deutschmarks. This put an enormous strain on businesses. Products that were highly coveted in the GDR and were even exported now became shelf warmers. What followed was, in the eyes of its critics, reckless destruction. For its advocates, it was a painful but unavoidable path to financial recovery.

10-01 „Sind wir schon verkauft?" steht 1990 am Zaun der Kaligrube „Glück auf" in Sondershausen (Thüringen), die von der Treuhandanstalt privatisiert werden soll.
"Have we been sold yet?" is written on the fence of the "Glück auf" potash mine in Sondershausen (Thuringia), which is due to be privatised by the Treuhandanstalt.

10-02 Mit einer Autobahnblockade protestieren Eisenacher Autobauer am 25. Januar 1991 gegen den von der Treuhand zum Monatsende verordneten Produktionsstopp des Pkw Wartburg.
On 25th January 1991, car factory workers in Eisenach protest against the Treuhand's decree to halt production in the Pkw Wartburg factory at the end of the month by blockading the autobahn.

10-03 Blick auf das Glaswerk in Jena, 1991. Die Sanierung des Volkseigenen Betriebes Carl Zeiss gehört zu den Erfolgsgeschichten der Treuhandanstalt.
View over the glass factory in Jena, 1991. The restructuring of the publicly-owned company Carl Zeiss is one of the biggest success stories of the Treuhandanstalt.

WARNUNG!

Mitarbeiter der Treuhandanstalt

betreten das Gebiet der Gemeinden
Siegelbach, Dosdorf u. Espenfeld
auf eigene Gefahr.

Köllmer, Bürgermeister

10-04 Am 1. April 1991 wird Treuhandchef Detlev Karsten Rohwedder in seinem Haus in Düsseldorf mutmaßlich
von RAF-Terroristen erschossen.
*On 1st April 1991, the director of the Treuhand, Detlev Karsten Rohwedder, is shot dead in his house in
Düsseldorf, the main suspects being Red Army Faction terrorists.*

10-05 Ein vom Bürgermeister gezeichnetes Schild warnt 1992 Mitarbeiter der Treuhandanstalt davor, drei
thüringische Gemeinden in der Nähe von Arnstadt zu betreten.
*In 1992, a signpost signed by the local mayor warns employees of the Treuhandanstalt against visiting
three communities near Arnstadt in Thuringia.*

10-06 „Treuhand, wie treu handelst du?" und „Schluß mit der VerKOHLerei" – Losungen der Stahlwerker
aus Hennigsdorf, die 1992 vor dem Sitz der Treuhand in Berlin protestieren.
*Steel workers from Hennigsdorf protesting outside the headquarters of the Treuhand in Berlin hold up
slogans such as "Treuhand, wie treu handelst du?" (roughly: "Trust Agency, how can we trust you?") and
"Schluß mit der VerKOHLerei" ("Enough of [Helmut] Kohl's meddling", a play on words – "verkohlen"
meaning "to take the mickey").*

10-07 Die Präsidentin der Treuhandanstalt Birgit Breuel besucht 1994 das Waschmittelwerk Genthin, das
1990 vom Henkel-Konzern übernommen wurde. Die Trümmer stammen von dem kurz zuvor
abgerissenen alten DDR-Werk.
*The President of the Treuhandanstalt, Birgit Breuel, visits the detergent factory in Genthin in 1994, which
was taken over by the Henkel Corporation in 1990. The rubble is from the recently demolished GDR
factory.*

VIDEO
Wie die Treuhand gearbeitet hat,
MDR 2015, 1:59 Min.

*How the Treuhand worked,
MDR 2015, 1:59 mins.*

VIDEO
Privatisierung – Im ländlichen Mecklenburg-Vor-
pommern wird die Landwirtschaft umgebaut. Die
Treuhand verwaltet auch die Vermögen der einst
Volkseigenen Güter (VEG), NDR 2019, 3:04 Min.

*Privatisation – Agriculture in rural Mecklenburg-Western
Pomerania is being transformed. The Treuhand also
manages the assets of the former Volkseigenes Gut farm
("Publicly Owned Estate"), NDR 2019, 3:04 mins.*

FRAUEN
WOMEN

Frauen in der DDR sind im Berufsleben bis zu den mittleren Leitungspositionen viel stärker präsent als ihre Geschlechtsgenossinnen im Westen. Neben der Berufstätigkeit haben sie außerdem die Lasten des aufreibenden Ostalltags zu tragen – allen voran die ständige Jagd nach Mangelwaren. Mit dem Umbruch von 1989 / 90 endet zwar der allgegenwärtige Mangel, dafür werden Frauen vielerorts als Erstes „abgewickelt". Zeitweilig gelten sie als Verliererinnen der Einheit, bis nach und nach deutlich wird, dass auffallend viele ostdeutsche Frauen beruflich und nicht zuletzt politisch aktiv und erfolgreich sind. Regine Hildebrandt wird als brandenburgische Sozialministerin zur Symbolfigur im Kampf um Gleichberechtigung – nicht nur der Frauen, sondern vieler Ostdeutscher. Und schließlich ist es Angela Merkel, die die Bundesrepublik seit 2005 erfolgreich führt und dafür international oft anhaltendere Anerkennung findet als zu Hause. Beiden gemeinsam ist, dass sie ihr Frausein als gegebene Selbstverständlichkeit empfinden, das keiner besonderen Erwähnung bedarf.

Working women in the GDR have a much stronger presence up to middle management level than their fellow women in the West. On top of their professional life, they also have to bear the brunt of gruelling everyday life in the East – and above all the constant hunt for scarce commodities. With the upheaval of 1989 / 90, the pervasive shortages come to an end, but women are in many places among the first to be "wound up". For a short time, they are among the biggest losers of reunification, until it gradually becomes clear that many former East German women are noticeably both professionally and politically active and successful. The Social Minister in Brandenburg, Regine Hildebrandt becomes a figurehead in the fight for equality – not only for women, but for many former East Germans too. And in the end it is Angela Merkel who successfully leads the Federal Republic for a decade and often finds more sustained recognition on the international stage than at home. One thing both women have in common is that they perceive their womanhood as self-evident and not worthy of any special mention.

11-01   Streikende Bergarbeiterinnen im Kalibergwerk Bischofferode.
Striking mine workers at the Bischofferode potash mine.

11-02   Straßenszene in Leipzig, 1991.
A street scene in Leipzig, 1991.

11-03   Die Übertragung des restriktiven westdeutschen Abtreibungsrechts auf die neuen Bundesländer sorgt nach der Wiedervereinigung unter ostdeutschen Frauen für Empörung. Foto: 1992
The introduction of restrictive West German abortion laws in the new federal states is met with outrage by East German women after the reunification. Photo: 1992

11-04 Momentaufnahme im Arbeitsamt Jena, 1994.
A snapshot in an employment office, Jena, 1994.

11-05 1990 wird in Leipzig mit Hansa Computer das erste Apple-Center in den neuen Bundesländern gegründet. Das Foto zeigt eine Mitarbeiterin der Firma 1993.
In 1990, the first Apple Center is founded in the new federal states in the form of Hansa Computer in Leipzig. The photo shows one of the company's employees in 1993.

11-06 Die Kindertagesstätte der TU Ilmenau 1994. Das dichte System der Kinderbetreuung aus DDR-Zeiten hilft vielen ostdeutschen Frauen, sich entgegen allen Widrigkeiten auf dem Arbeitsmarkt zu behaupten.
The daycare centre at the Technical University Ilmenau in 1994. The airtight system of childcare from the days of the GDR helps many East German women to hold their ground in the world of work despite all the adversities.

11-07 Angela Merkel, Bundesministerin für Frauen und Jugend (rechts), und Regine Hildebrandt, Ministerin für Arbeit, Soziales, Gesundheit und Frauen des Landes Brandenburg (links), treffen sich am Rande der 1. Gleichstellungsministerkonferenz 1991 in Potsdam.
Angela Merkel, Federal Minister for Women and Youth (right) and Regine Hildebrandt, Minister for Work, Social Affairs, Health and Women for the State of Brandenburg (left), meet on the sidelines of the 1st Ministerial Conference on Equality in Potsdam in 1991.

VIDEO
Ostfrauen in der Bundesregierung, Animationsfilm, entstanden im Rahmen des Projekts Ostfrauen von RBB und MDR, © Hoferichter & Jacobs 2019, 1:01 Min.

Ostfrauen in der Bundesregierung, Animationsfilm, entstanden im Rahmen des Projekts Ostfrauen von RBB und MDR, © Hoferichter & Jacobs 2019, 1:01 Min.

VIDEO
Gleichberechtigung – Beruf und Familie unter einem
Hut? Für Frauen im Osten ist das seit den 1960er
Jahren eine Selbstverständlichkeit, anders als in
Westdeutschland, NDR 2019, 3:12 Min.
*Equality – A job and a family at the same time? For women
in the East, this was a matter of course from the 1960s
onwards, unlike in West Germany, NDR 2019, 3:12 mins.*

UM WO
BRUCH UM
OST 12

SANIERUNG
RENOVATION

Versetzen wir uns in eine jener hübschen Kleinstädte Ostdeutschlands, deren Rathäuser und Marktplätze vom Gewerbefleiß zeugen, der dort über Jahrhunderte für Wohlstand gesorgt hat. Die alten Fassaden sind liebevoll restauriert, die Zunftzeichen über den Läden, der Apotheke und dem Ratskeller frisch vergoldet. Vor einem Café sitzen ältere Damen und plaudern angeregt. Sofern sie schon länger hier wohnen, können sie sich noch daran erinnern, wie der Stadtkern 1989 ausgesehen hat: Regenrinnen hingen herab, Wasser fraß sich ins Gemäuer und Dachziegel fielen Passanten zuweilen auf den Kopf. In den 1980er Jahren standen ganze Stadtviertel vor dem Abriss, um gesichtslosen Neubauten Platz zu machen. Und die Bewohner wehrten sich nicht, weil sie hofften, endlich selbst eine Wohnung mit Bad und Fernheizung zu bekommen. Seit der Wiedervereinigung sind nicht nur die historischen Innenstädte, sondern ist die gesamte Infrastruktur Ostdeutschlands mit Fördergeldern in Milliardenhöhe aufwendig saniert worden. Bei vielen Menschen ist die Erinnerung an die mausgraue Tristesse des DDR-Alltags mehr und mehr verblasst.

Let us imagine ourselves in one of those sweet little towns in former East Germany whose town halls and marketplaces are testament to the industriousness that ensured prosperity for centuries. The old façades have been lovingly restored, the guild signs above the shops, pharmacies and the town hall's bar have been freshly gilded. Elderly women sit in front of a café, chatting excitedly. If they have lived here for a long time, they will still remember what the town centre looked like in 1989. Gutters drooped from the roofs, water seeped into the walls and roof tiles occasionally came crashing down on passers-by. In the 1980s, entire neighbourhoods were in danger of being torn down to make space for faceless new buildings. The locals put up no struggle in the hope that they might finally be given their own apartment with a bath and central heating. Following the reunification, not only historic town centres but the entire infrastructure of former East Germany is extensively renovated with aid money running into the billions. Many people find that memories of the mouse-grey dreariness of everyday life in the GDR start to fade away.

12-01 Blick auf restaurierte Fachwerkhäuser im Zentrum von Quedlinburg (Sachsen-Anhalt), 2004. Die Stadt wird 1994 von der UNESCO zum Weltkulturerbe erklärt.
A view of restored timber-framed houses in the centre of Quedlinburg (Saxony-Anhalt), 2004. The town is declared a world heritage site by UNESCO in 1994.

12-02 Quedlinburg im Jahre 1990.
Quedlinburg in the year 1990.

12-03 Am Niedersachsenplatz in Halle-Neustadt werden im Juli 2004 Plattenbauten abgerissen. Die Einwohnerzahl von Halle ist in den 14 Jahren nach der Wiedervereinigung um rund 70.000 auf 237.000 Bürger geschrumpft.
Prefabricated high-rises are demolished on Niedersachsenplatz in Halle-Neustadt in July 2004. The number of inhabitants in Halle shrank by around 70,000 to 237,000 residents in the 14 years after the reunification.

12-04 Die Mainzer Straße in Berlin-Friedrichshain im Sommer 1990. Seit dem Mauerfall besetzten junge Leute in ostdeutschen Großstädten leerstehende Altbauten. Im November 1990 lässt der Berliner Senat die Mainzer Straße räumen. Es kommt zu Straßenschlachten.
Mainzer Straße in Berlin-Friedrichshain in the summer of 1990. After the fall of the Berlin Wall, young people occupy empty old buildings in various East German cities. In November 1990, the Berlin Senate orders Mainzer Straße to be cleared. Street fighting breaks out.

12-05 In den 1990er Jahren prägen Baukräne das Bild ostdeutscher Städte. Eine Gruppe von Managern begutachtet den Baufortschritt auf dem Debis-Gelände am Potsdamer Platz, Frühjahr 1994.
In the 1990s, construction cranes dominate the skylines of East German cities. A group of managers assesses the construction progress on the debis site at Potsdamer Platz, spring 1994.

12-06 Beim Ausbau der BAB 4 bei Chemnitz muss unter dem 1872 errichteten denkmalgeschützten Eisenbahnviadukt ein tunnelartiger Bau für die Fahrbahnverbreiterung gebaut werden. Foto: 2001.
During the upgrading of the Bundesautobahn 4 near Chemnitz, a tunnel had to be built under the listed railway viaduct dating from 1872 to allow the carriageway to be widened. Photo: 2001.

12-07 An der Ruine der Dresdner Frauenkirche wird 1992 deren Wiederaufbau angekündigt.
Plans to rebuild Dresden's Frauenkirche are displayed in front of the ruins in 1992.

VIDEO
Christoph Trebbin: Einstürzende Altbauten, zeitzeugen-portal.de, 8:19 Min.

Christoph Trebbin: Collapsing old buildings, zeitzeugen-portal.de, 8:19 mins.

VIDEO
Farbenlehre – Graue, verfallene Altbauten prägen
nach 1989 noch etliche Jahre die ostdeutschen
Innenstädte. Wer damals geboren wird, wächst in
einer sich allmählich ändernden Farbenwelt auf,
NDR 2019, 1:55 Min.

*Colour theory – Grey, derelict old buildings still
characterise East German inner cities many years after
1989. Those born at this time grow up in a gradually
developing world of colour, NDR 2019, 1:55 mins.*

UM WO
BRUCH UM
OST '13

VERLUSTE
LOSSES

Zwischen Ostseeküste und Fichtelgebirge trotzen bis heute einige Bücherstuben tapfer der Übermacht der sterilen Filialen von Buchhandelsketten mit ihren vakuumverpackten Bestsellern. Viele von ihnen haben ein antiquarisches Angebot, und dort riecht es wirklich noch nach Osten – im übertragenen wie im buchstäblichen Sinne: traulich, verstaubt, gemütlich, leicht modrig und ungelüftet. In den vollgestopften Bücherregalen haben sich die Epochen der Geschichte abgelagert wie die geologischen Formationen des Erdmantels. In den Regalen lässt sich eine Tektonik erkennen, die viel von der Geschichte jenes Ländchens hinter der Mauer erzählt. Dem Kenner entgehen die Lücken nicht, doch beeindruckt die inhaltliche Vielgestaltigkeit der äußerlich angestaubten und vergilbten Bücher. Dort liegt der Lesestoff, der damals so schwer zu bekommen war. Spätestens bei den Kinder- und Jugendbüchern wird der Kunde schwach und investiert zwei oder drei Euro für die verlorenen Träume der Jugend.

To this day, there are some bookshops between the Baltic coast and Fichtel Mountains which bravely defy the dominance of the sterile branches of bookstore chains with their vacuum-packed best-sellers. Many of them have second-hand offerings and the shops themselves really do still invoke the former East – both figuratively and literally: cosy, dusty, unhurried, slightly musty and unventilated. Whole eras of history have been deposited on the crowded bookshelves like the geological formations of the earth's crust. These shelves contain an archive that explains a great deal about the history of that little country behind the wall. The gaps do not go unnoticed to the trained eye, but the wide-ranging content of the superficially dusty and yellowed books is still impressive. They include reading material that was hard to come by at the time. Customers yearn particularly for children's books and part with two or three euros for the lost dreams of their youth.

13-01 „Die DDR hat's nie gegeben" steht im Dezember 2008 an einer Wand – dahinter die Brache, auf der der Palast der Republik gestanden hat. Dessen Abriss sorgt für heftige Debatten.
„Die DDR hat's nie gegeben" (meaning "The GDR never existed") is scrawled on a wall in December 2008 – behind it is the wasteland on which the Palace of the Republic stood. Its demolition triggered a heated debate.

13-02 Eine Buchhandlung verramscht Bücher aus der DDR. Foto: 1991.
A bookshop sells off books from the GDR at a loss. Photo: 1991.

13-03 Seit 1990 sammelt der Schauspieler Peter Sodann Bücher aus der DDR. Seine Sammlung ist mittlerweile auf über 600.000 Bände angewachsen. Foto: 2011.
The actor Peter Sodann has collected books from the GDR since 1990. His collection has now grown to more than 600,000 volumes. Photo: 2011.

13-04 In Relation zur Einwohnerzahl gibt es 1988 in der DDR viermal mehr öffentliche Bibliotheken als in der Bundesrepublik. In den 1990er Jahren werden in Ostdeutschland viele Bibliotheken geschlossen. Das liegt nicht nur am Geld – anders als in der DDR sind nun alle Bücher im Handel jederzeit verfügbar. Foto: 1996.
In relation to the number of inhabitants, in 1988 there are four times as many public libraries in East Germany as in the West. Many libraries in the GDR are closed during the 1990s. This is not only for financial reasons – unlike in the GDR, all books are now commercially available. Photo: 1996.

13-05 1999 wird in Weimar die Ausstellung „Aufstieg und Fall der Moderne" gezeigt, der vorgeworfen wird, die Kunst der DDR zu diffamieren.
An exhibition called "Aufstieg und Fall der Moderne" ("The Rise and Fall of Modernity") was held in Weimar in 1999, which was accused of defaming art from the GDR.

13-06 Trauerfeier für die verstorbene Autorin Christa Wolf am 13. Dezember 2011 in Berlin. Die Schriftstellerin war in den 1990er Jahren wegen einer kurzzeitigen Mitarbeit für das MfS attackiert worden.
A memorial service for the deceased author Christa Wolf on 13th December 2011 in Berlin. The writer was criticised for having worked for a short time for the GDR's Ministry of State Security in the 1990s.

13-07 Musiker der Mecklenburgischen Staatskapelle protestieren 2013 gegen den Stellenabbau im Kulturbetrieb.
Musicians from the Mecklenburgische Staatskapelle protest against job cuts in the cultural sector in 2013.

VIDEO
DDR-Kunst neu gesehen,
Deutsche Welle TV, 5:46 Min.

GDR art in a new light,
Deutsche Welle TV, 5:46 mins.

Wir haben
sie, die
Ost-Schrippe
-,28

Mischbrot

OSTALGIE
OSTALGIE

In den neunziger Jahren beginnt der Siegeszug der Ostschrippe. Natürlich kostet die dann schon lange keine fünf Pfennige mehr. Doch um den Preis geht es bei diesem Symbol der Ostalgie gar nicht so sehr. Die Ostschrippe kommt direkt aus dem Ofen. Sie ist zwar klein, aber knusprig, also irgendwie ehrlich und bodenständig – genauso, wie sich der Ostler sieht. Das Westbrötchen dagegen ist künstlich aufgeblasen und mit Kinkerlitzchen angereichert. Es heißt auch nicht mehr Schrippe, sondern gibt sich als Bioprodukt oder französisch vornehm als Baguette. Und teurer ist es auch noch. Könnte man eine schönere Metapher für den Westler finden? Da mag man nichts davon hören, dass die stark subventionierten DDR-Schrippen mancherorts als billiges Futtermittel an Hühner und Schweine gingen. Oder dass die Bäcker der Not gehorchend bis 1989 oft zu Ersatzstoffen greifen mussten. Mythen sind unsterblich und lassen sich nur schwer durch Fakten widerlegen.

The 1990s see the beginning of the triumph of the Ostschrippe. Of course, it does not take long for the price to rise from the original five pfennigs. However, the price is not the most important thing about this symbol of Ostalgie. The Ostschrippe comes straight out of the oven. It is admittedly small, but crispy, and somehow honest and down-to-earth – just how former Easterners see themselves. A Western bread roll, conversely, is artificially inflated and enhanced with odds and ends. It is not called a Schrippe any more either, but is presented as an organic product, or preferably in French as a baguette. It is more expensive as well. Is there a more apt metaphor for those who East Germans colloquially called "Westler"? East Germans do not want to hear of how heavily subsidised GDR Schrippen were used in some places as cheap animal feed for chickens and pigs. Or of how bakers had to give in to necessity and use substitute ingredients in the years prior to 1989. Myths are immortal and not easy to refute with facts.

14-01   In einem Bäckerladen in der Husemannstraße in Berlin-Prenzlauer Berg wird 1994 ein Korb frischer „Ost-Schrippen" angeboten.
A basket of fresh "Ost-Schrippen" bread is offered in a bakery in Husemannstraße in Berlin-Prenzlauer Berg, 1994.

14-02   Ein besetztes Haus in Potsdam, 1991. Bis 1989 Pflichtübung, wird die Beflaggung mit Hammer, Zirkel und Ährenkranz zu einem leicht verfügbaren Statement, das immer für eine Provokation gut ist.
An occupied house in Potsdam, 1991. An obligatory act up until 1989, the flags adorned with a hammer, a sickle and a circle of rye became an easily obtainable statement that always served as a provocation.

14-03   Dieter Hertrampf und Dieter Birr von den Puhdys sowie Karat-Leadsänger Herbert Dreilich bei einem Auftritt 1992. Mit wachsendem Abstand zur DDR steigt die Popularität der alten DDR-Bands.
Dieter Hertrampf and Dieter Birr from the Puhdys, along with the leader singer of Karat, Herbert Dreilich, at a performance in 1992. As more time passed since the end of the GDR, old GDR bands grew in popularity.

14-04 Die Verbrauchermesse OSTPRO findet 1993 im Pavillon am Fuße des Berliner Fernsehturms statt. Das Mekka der Ostprodukte bietet Nachschub an Badusan, Nudossi und Co.
The OSTPRO consumer trade fair for 1993 is held in the pavilion at the base of Berlin's television tower. The mecca for products from the East offers a boost to Badusan, Nudossi and others.

14-05 Ostalgie-Party in Berlin, 1994.
Ostalgie party in Berlin, 1994.

14-06 Espenhain, 1997: Der Trabi wird geputzt. Mittlerweile hat das Plastikauto wieder neue Liebhaber gefunden.
Espenhain, 1997: a Trabant owner cleans her car. The plastic car won more new fans after the GDR's collapse.

14-07 „Wessis aufs Maul" steht 2011 an der Bahnhofswand in Groß Kiesow in Mecklenburg-Vorpommern.
"Wessis aufs Maul": a message threatening violence against West Germans is graffitied across a wall of the railway station in Groß Kiesow in Mecklenburg-Western Pomerania, 2011.

VIDEO
Hans-Jürgen Krieger: Rückbesinnung auf Ost-Produkte, zeitzeugen-portal.de, 4:34 Min.

Hans-Jürgen Krieger: Recollecting old East German products, zeitzeugen-portal.de, 4:34 mins.

VIDEO

Sehnsucht – Es war nicht alles schlecht: Mit wachsendem Abstand wird das Bild der DDR in vielen Familienerzählungen immer farbenfroher, NDR 2019, 3:26 Min.

Yearning – It wasn't all bad: as more time goes by, family recollections of the GDR become ever more colourful, NDR 2019, 3:26 mins.

Bildungschancen / Education opportunities

Thüringen bei Abi-Noten vorne
Ausgewählte Daten zu Bildung und Berufseinstieg

Thuringia tops the table in Abitur grades
Selected statistics on education and career entry

■ Durchschnittliche Abiturnoten 2016 / 2017 | Average Abitur grades (secondary school leaving exam) 2016 / 2017
■ Anteil der Studienanfänger* 2017 | Proportion of new students* 2017
■ Arbeitslosenquote 15 bis unter 25 Jahre September 2019 | Unemployment rate among young people aged 15–25 September 2019

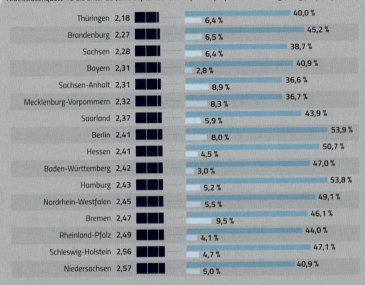

Land	Abiturnote	Arbeitslosenquote	Studienanfänger
Thüringen	2,18	40,0 %	6,4 %
Brandenburg	2,27	45,2 %	6,5 %
Sachsen	2,28	38,7 %	6,4 %
Bayern	2,31	40,9 %	2,8 %
Sachsen-Anhalt	2,31	36,6 %	8,9 %
Mecklenburg-Vorpommern	2,32	36,7 %	8,3 %
Saarland	2,37	43,9 %	5,9 %
Berlin	2,41	53,9 %	8,0 %
Hessen	2,41	50,7 %	4,5 %
Baden-Württemberg	2,42	47,0 %	3,0 %
Hamburg	2,43	53,8 %	5,2 %
Nordrhein-Westfalen	2,45	49,1 %	5,5 %
Bremen	2,47	46,1 %	9,5 %
Rheinland-Pfalz	2,49	44,0 %	4,1 %
Schleswig-Holstein	2,56	47,1 %	4,7 %
Niedersachsen	2,57	40,9 %	5,0 %

* an der Bevölkerung des entsprechenden Geburtsjahres | of the population born in the same year

---

Geld und Freundschaft / Money and friendship

Frau Ost und Frau West werden im selben Alter Mütter
Durchschnittliches Alter der Mütter bei der Geburt ihres ersten Kindes

Women in former East and West Germany become mothers at the same age
Average age of the mother upon the birth of her first child

● Ostdeutschland*
Former East Germany*

● Westdeutschland
Former West Germany

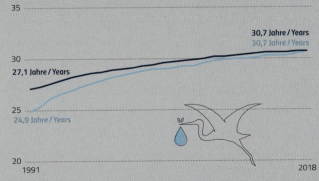

30,7 Jahre / Years
30,7 Jahre / Years

27,1 Jahre / Years

24,9 Jahre / Years

35

30

25

20

1991   2018

* neue Länder inkl. Berlin-Ost, ab 2001 ohne Berlin | states of former East Germany including East Berlin, but excluding Berlin from 2001

So viel können Jugendliche ausgeben
Geldbetrag, der Jugendlichen pro Monat für Konsum und Sparen zur Verfügung steht

How much young people can spend
Amount of money that young people have available to save and spend each month

445 € Bremen
401 € Baden-Württemberg
397 € Rheinland-Pfalz
381 € Hamburg
378 € Brandenburg

376 € Nordrhein-Westfalen
368 € Hessen
367 € Sachsen
362 € Deutschland
359 € Berlin
354 € Thüringen

343 € Schleswig-Holstein
338 € Saarland
329 € Niedersachsen
327 € Mecklenburg-Vorpommern
322 € Bayern
303 € Sachsen-Anhalt

Basis: 1.600 Befragte von 16–25 Jahren, Januar 2019 | Base: 1,600 respondents aged 16–25, January 2019

Sachsen-Anhalter und Schleswig-Holsteiner sind am ungeselligsten
Anteil der Befragten, die sehr / eher häufig Freunde, Bekannte oder Arbeitskollegen treffen

Young people in Saxony-Anhalt and Schleswig-Holstein are the least sociable
Proportion of respondents who meet up with friends, acquaintances or work colleagues very / fairly often

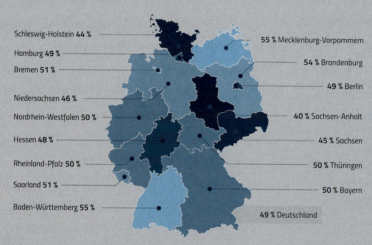

Schleswig-Holstein 44 %
Hamburg 49 %
Bremen 51 %
Niedersachsen 46 %
Nordrhein-Westfalen 50 %
Hessen 48 %
Rheinland-Pfalz 50 %
Saarland 51 %
Baden-Württemberg 55 %

55 % Mecklenburg-Vorpommern
54 % Brandenburg
49 % Berlin
40 % Sachsen-Anhalt
45 % Sachsen
50 % Thüringen
50 % Bayern
49 % Deutschland

Basis: 4.968 Befragte; 2017 | Base: 4,968 respondents; 2017

Heute heiratet Frau Ost später als Frau West
Alter bei Heirat von Frauen in Deutschland

Women in former East Germany marry later than those in the West
Marrying age of women in Germany

* ab 1990 ohne Berlin | not including Berlin from 1990   ** ab 1990 einschließlich Berlin | including Berlin from 1990

Ostehen stabiler als früher
Scheidungen je 10.000 bestehende Ehen

Marriages in former East Germany are more stable than before
Separations per 10,000 married couples

*   ab 1990 ohne Berlin | excluding Berlin from 1990
** ab 1990 einschließlich Berlin | including Berlin from 1990

Jugendliche in Ostdeutschland sind empfänglicher für Populismus
Anteil der Jugendlichen die ...

Young people in former East Germany are more receptive to populism
Proportion of young people who...

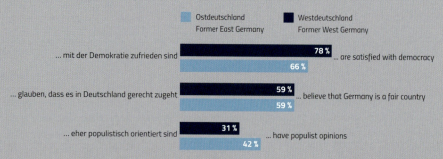

Ostdeutschland
Former East Germany

Westdeutschland
Former West Germany

... mit der Demokratie zufrieden sind — 78 % ... are satisfied with democracy
66 %

... glauben, dass es in Deutschland gerecht zugeht — 59 % ... believe that Germany is a fair country
59 %

... eher populistisch orientiert sind — 31 % ... have populist opinions
42 %

Basis: 2.572 Jugendliche (12–25 Jahre) in Deutschland; Januar–März 2019
Base: 2,572 young people (aged 12–25) in Germany; January–March 2019

So (un)politisch ist die Jugend in Deutschland
Anteil der Jugendlichen in Deutschland, die sich für Politik interessieren

Political (in)activity among young people in Germany
Proportion of young people in Germany who are interested in politics

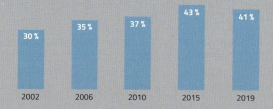

2002	2006	2010	2015	2019
30 %	35 %	37 %	43 %	41 %

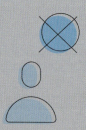

Basis: 2.572 Befragte von 12–25 Jahren; 2019 | Base: 2,572 respondents aged 12–25; 2019

Quellen: Bertelsmann Stiftung, Bundesagentur für Arbeit, Bundeszentrale für gesundheitliche Aufklärung, comdirect Bank, Kultusministerkonferenz, Shell Jugendstudie, Statistisches Bundesamt.
Sources: Bertelsmann Foundation, Federal Labour Office, Federal Centre for Health Education, comdirect Bank, Standing Conference of the Ministers of Education and Cultural Affairs, Shell Youth Study, Federal Statistical Office.
Design: Cecilia Rojas, Anne Geick, Miriam Kaiser.

RECHTSRADIKALISMUS
RIGHT-WING EXTREMISM

Tief im Osten von Berlin liegt die Weitlingstraße. Die unansehnliche Vorstadtstraße kommt Anfang der neunziger Jahre als Hochburg der rechtsradikalen Nationalen Alternative zu traurigem Ruhm. In schlimmster sprachlicher Tradition beschimpfen Jungnazis ihre Gegner als „Zecken". Für Ausländer und Linke wird die Gegend zum gefährlichen Pflaster. Diese seltsame Sumpfblüte der Friedlichen Revolution ist tatsächlich ein originäres DDR-Gewächs. Doch wie kann es sein, dass nach vierzig Jahren Erziehung zum Antifaschismus, zur Völkerfreundschaft und zur internationalen Solidarität ein Teil der ostdeutschen Jugend sich Glatzen scheren lässt und mit Springerstiefeln zum „Zeckenklatschen" loszieht? Allein die Freude an der Provokation kann es kaum sein. Offenbar hat unter der Decke der Solidaritätsparolen immer ein rechtes Potenzial geschlummert, das sich Anfang der neunziger Jahre Bahn bricht. Als in Rostock-Lichtenhagen das Wohnheim der Vietnamesen brennt und der aufgestachelte Mob Beifall klatscht, sind dort keineswegs nur „Glatzen" zu sehen.

Deep in the East of Berlin is Weitlingstraße. This unprepossessing suburban street develops an unhappy reputation in the early 90s as a stronghold of the extreme right-wing group Nationale Alternative. In the worst linguistic tradition, young Nazis insult their opponents by calling them "Zecken" (ticks). The area becomes dangerous for foreigners and leftists. This strange, evil tumour of the peaceful revolution in fact originated in the GDR. But how can it be that after forty years of education against fascism and in favour of international friendship and solidarity, part of East Germany's youth can shave their heads, don combat boots and start shouting extremist abuse? It can hardly be merely the enjoyment of provocation. Behind the veneer of the language of solidarity, the potential for a right-wing resurgence was evidently slumbering, which then broke free in the early 90s. In Rostock-Lichtenhagen, when the apartment block housing Vietnamese immigrants burns, the assembled, applauding mob is made up of more than just skinheads.

15-01 Ingo Hasselbach, der später als Aussteiger aus der Neonazi-Szene Bekanntheit erlangen wird, 1992 beim Plakatekleben am Bahnhof Lichtenberg in Berlin.
Ingo Hasselbach, who would later gain recognition as a dropout of the neo-Nazi scene, sticking up posters in Lichtenberg Railway Station in Berlin in 1992.

15-02 Nach ausländerfeindlichen Übergriffen werden im September 1991 Flüchtlinge unter Polizeischutz in Bussen aus Hoyerswerda (Sachsen) evakuiert.
Following xenophobic assaults, refugees are evacuated in buses from Hoyerswerda (Saxony) with a police escort, September 1991.

15-03 Sächsische Neonazis feiern am 17. November 1991 Hoyerswerda als die „erste ausländerfreie Stadt Deutschlands".
On 17th November 1991, neo-Nazis in Saxony celebrate Hoyerswerda becoming the "first foreigner-free town in Germany".

15-04   Brandanschlag auf ein Asylbewerberheim im Dorf Dolgenbrodt in Brandenburg, 1997.
An arson attack on a refugee centre in the village of Dolgenbrodt in Brandenburg, 1997.

15-05   1992: Kundgebung gegen fremdenfeindliche Gewalt vor dem Brandenburger Tor in Berlin.
Demonstranten tragen Schilder mit den Namen der Orte, an denen rechtsradikale Anschläge
verübt wurden.
*1992: a rally against xenophobic violence in front of the Brandenburg Gate in Berlin. Demonstrators
hold signs with the names of places where extremist right-wing attacks had taken place.*

15-06   Politische Kontraste: Aufmarsch der rechtsextremen NPD im September 1998 in Rostock.
Am Laternenpfahl ein Wahlplakat der PDS.
*Political contrasts: a march organised by the extreme right-wing NPD (National Democratic Party
of Germany) in September 1998 in Rostock. Attached to the lamppost is an election poster for the
far-left PDS (Party of Democratic Socialism).*

15-07   An der Wand des stillgelegten Bahnhofs von Espenhain steht 1993 neben einem Hakenkreuz
„Gedanken kann man nicht verbieten".
*An abandoned railway station in Espenhain 1993: Next to the swastika is written "Gedanken kann
man nicht verbieten", meaning "Thoughts cannot be prohibited".*

- -

VIDEO
Martin Dulig: Jugend für Jugend,
zeitzeugen-portal.de, 5:43 Min.

*Martin Dulig: Young people for young
people, zeitzeugen-portal.de, 5:43 mins.*

- -

VIDEO

Rechtsruck – Die Fernsehbilder vom brennenden
Sonnenblumenhaus in Rostock-Lichtenhagen 1992
schockieren und werden zu einem bis heute fort-
wirkenden Symbol, NDR 2019, 3:51 Min.

A swing to the right – The TV images of the burning
Sonnenblumenhaus in Rostock-Lichtenhagen in 1992
shock viewers and become a symbol that continues to
have an effect to this day, NDR 2019, 3:51 mins.

UM WU
BRUCH
OST 16

JUGENDKULTUREN
YOUTH CULTURES

Nirgendwo ist die neue Freiheit in den neunziger Jahren deutlicher zu spüren als in Berlin. Dafür steht symbolisch das legendäre Tacheles – das Künstlerhaus in einer kriegszerstörten Kaufhausruine im Herzen Berlins. Die schrille Szene in dem wild bemalten Gebäude mit zahllosen Ausstellungen, Happenings und Konzerten gedeiht mit dem Geld des Berliner Senats. Das Zauberwort heißt Arbeitsbeschaffungsmaßnahme. In leer stehenden Fabrikhallen und andernorts entwickelt sich eine Partyszene, und ab 1989 zieht jährlich die Loveparade zu Technoklängen durch Berlin. Das Motto der als politische Demonstration angemeldeten Veranstaltung lautet „Friede, Freude, Eierkuchen". Konkreter wird es auch in den Folgejahren nicht. Die Loveparade wird zum Massenevent und zunehmend kommerzialisiert, bis sie aus Berlin nach Duisburg zieht und 2010 nach einer Massenpanik mit 21 Todesopfern eingestellt wird. Heute erzählen die Veteranen der Bewegung von einer Zeit mit unglaublichen Freiräumen, viel Spaß und lauter Musik.

Nowhere is the new freedom felt more tangibly than in Berlin during the 1990s. The legendary Tacheles, the art house in the ruins of a department store in the heart of Berlin, is symbolic of this. The eccentric scene in the gaudily painted building with numerous exhibitions, happenings and concerts thrives with money from the Senate of Berlin. The magic words that clinch the deal are "job creation". A party scene develops in vacant factory buildings and elsewhere, and from 1989 the Love Parade snakes through Berlin each year to the sound of techno music. The motto of the parade, which is registered as a political demonstration, is "Friede, Freude, Eierkuchen" (lit. 'peace, joy, pancakes', referring to problems being glossed over). Things do not take on any more definite form in the years that follow either. The Love Parade becomes a mass event and is increasingly commercialised, until it eventually moves from Berlin to Duisburg and is discontinued in 2010 after a mass panic results in 21 deaths. Today, veterans of the movement speak of a time with incredible freedom, a lot of fun and loud music.

16-01 Die 1990er Jahre sind die Blütezeit der Technomusik, die Berliner Loveparade wird zum alljährlichen Höhepunkt einer eigenen Jugendkultur. Foto: 1996.
The 1990s are the heyday of techno music, and the Berlin Love Parade becomes the annual highlight of the city's youth culture. Photo: 1996.

16-02 Derweil herrscht für viele Jugendliche fern der großen Zentren Langeweile und Orientierungslosigkeit. Leinefelde (Thüringen) 1997.
Meanwhile, many young people far from big cities suffer boredom and a lack of direction Leinefelde (Thuringia) 1997.

16-03 Skater-Park in Magdeburg-Olvenstedt, 1997.
A skate park in Magdeburg-Olvenstedt, 1997.

16-04 Leipzig, Dresden, vor allem aber Berlin sind Anziehungspunkte für Jugendliche, die die neuen Freiräume austesten wollen. Das Foto zeigt eine Wagenburg auf der Ostseite der einstigen Berliner Mauer, 1992.
Leipzig, Dresden and in particular Berlin are magnets for young people who want to test out their new-found freedom. The photo shows a group of vans on the eastern side of the former Berlin Wall, 1992.

16-05 Im Februar 1990 besetzt eine Künstlerinitiative die Ruine eines alten Kaufhauses in der Ost-Berliner Innenstadt. Daraus entsteht das Künstlerhaus Tacheles, das bis 2012 ein Besuchermagnet ist. Foto: 1992.
In February 1990, an art initiative occupies the ruins of a former department store in the centre of former East Berlin. It develops into the Art House Tacheles, which is a magnet for visitors until 2012. Photo: 1992.

16-06 Jugendweihe im Mai 1992. Die Jugendkultur der 1990er Jahre ist durch eine politische Polarisierung geprägt. Wer sich dem entzieht, sitzt – insbesondere in Kleinstädten – oft zwischen Baum und Borke.
A Jugendweihe (meaning "youth ceremony") in May 1992. The youth culture of the 1990s is characterised by political polarisation. Those who evade it often find themselves – especially in small towns – between a rock and a hard place.

16-07 Ein Techno-Tänzer bei der Job-Parade, die vom Deutschen Gewerkschaftsbund in Anlehnung an die Berliner Lovepa-rade am 1. Mai 1998 in Schwerin organisiert wurde. Motto: „Youth can't wait".
A techno dancer at the Job Parade in Schwerin, which was organised by the Federation of German Trade Unions in the style of the Berlin Love Parade and held on 1st May 1998. Its motto was "Youth can't wait".

VIDEO
Tokio Hotel – Pop-Idole und Wende-Kinder,
DW TV, 3:40 Min.

*Tokyo Hotel – Pop idols and children of the
reunification, DW TV, 3:40 mins.*

VIDEO

Freiheit – Für ostdeutsche Jugendliche scheinen die
Möglichkeiten nach 1989 schier grenzenlos zu sein.
Nur ... was anfangen mit der neu gewonnenen
Freiheit? NDR 2019, 3:03 Min.

*Freedom – For young people in post-1989 East Germany,
the opportunities seem endless. The question is... what
should we do with this newly gained freedom? NDR 2019,
3:03 mins.*

VEREINT
UNITED

Die Einheitseuphorie von 1990 verklingt nach und nach. Zwischen Ost und West fremdelt es immer häufiger. Ausgerechnet eine Flutkatastrophe lässt Deutschland wieder zusammenrücken. Am 17. Juli 1997 erreicht die Oderflut das Land Brandenburg. Dauerregen hat die Deiche zusätzlich aufgeweicht. Bei Brieskow-Finkenheerd bricht der Damm, und die Wassermassen überschwemmen die Ernst-Thälmann-Siedlung. In Frankfurt (Oder) erreicht der Pegel am 27. Juli mit 6,57 Metern Rekordhöhe. Der schützende Sandsackdamm ist nur noch wenige Zentimeter höher. Vorsorglich wird im nördlichen Oderbruch die Evakuierung von 6.500 Menschen angeordnet. Doch viele bleiben und füllen zusammen mit den Soldaten der Bundeswehr Tag und Nacht Sandsäcke, um die Bruchstellen im Damm zu schließen. Aus allen Bundesländern kommen Spenden und oft mehr freiwillige Helfer, als gebraucht werden. Von der Wasserseite wird der Deich von Tauchern mit Folien abgedeckt. Dann sinkt der Wasserstand, das Oderbruch ist gerettet und die große Gemeinschaftsaktion wird zur Legende.

The euphoria of reunification fades away gradually after 1990. Residents of the former East and West are increasingly wary of each other. Of all things, it is a catastrophic flood that brings Germany closer together again. On 17th July 1997, the Oder Flood reaches the state of Brandenburg. Incessant rain has put even more strain on the dykes. A dam near Brieskow-Finkenheerd breaks and the body of water inundates the Ernst-Thälmann estate. In Frankfurt an der Oder, the River Pegel reaches a record height of 6.57 metres on 27th July. The protective sandbag embankment is just a few centimetres taller. An evacuation of 6,500 people is ordered as a preventative measure in the northern part of Oderbruch. However, many stay behind and work day and night with soldiers from the Bundeswehr to fill sandbags, which are used to close up breaches in the dam. Donations come in from all the other federal states and often more volunteers than are needed. Divers pull sheets across the water side of the dam. The waters recede, Oderbruch is saved and the huge community effort becomes a legend.

17-01 Bundeswehrsoldaten verstärken am 27. Juli 1997 in Frankfurt (Oder) einen Schutzdeich mit Sandsäcken.
Bundeswehr soldiers reinforce a protective embankment with sandbags on 27th July 1997 in Frankfurt an der Oder.

17-02 Die überflutete Ernst-Thälmann-Siedlung in der Nähe von Ziltendorf in Brandenburg, am 27. Juli 1997.
The flooded Ernst-Thälmann estate near Ziltendorf in Brandenburg. Photo: 27th July 1997.

17-03 Bundeswehrsoldaten arbeiten 1997 Hand in Hand mit zivilen Helfern im überfluteten Ratzdorf an der deutsch-polnischen Grenze.
Bundeswehr soldiers work hand in hand with civilian volunteers in flooded Ratzdorf on the German-Polish border, 1997.

17-04 Passau, 12. August 2002: Es kommt erneut zu einer Flutkatastrophe in Österreich, Tschechien und Deutschland.
Passau, 12th August 2002: Another flooding catastrophe affects Austria, the Czech Republic and Germany.

17-05 Fünf Tage später ist die historische Altstadt von Dresden überflutet.
Five days later, the historic Old Town of Dresden is flooded.

17-06 Die westdeutsche Fußball-Legende Paul Breitner mit dem Trikot, in dem DDR-Nationalspieler Jürgen Sparwasser 1971 bei der Fußball-WM den 1:0-Siegtreffer erzielte. Das Trikot wird am 18. August 2002 zugunsten der Flutopfer versteigert.
West German football legend Paul Breitner with the shirt in which GDR-national Jürgen Sparwasser scored the winning goal in a 1:0 victory for the East at the World Cup in 1971. The shirt is auctioned on 18th August 2002 with proceeds going to victims of the flooding.

17-07 ZDF-Benefizkonzert zugunsten der Flutopfer am 3. September 2002 vor der Semperoper in Dresden.
A ZDF charity concert on 3rd September 2002 in front of the Semper Opera House in Dresden in support of victims of the flooding.

· ·

VIDEO
Jahresrückblick 1997 – Oder-Hochwasser,
tagesschau.de, 3:15 Min.

*Looking back at 1997 – The Central European
flood, tagesschau.de, 3:15 mins.*

· ·

VIDEO
Ossi oder Wessi? – In den ersten Jahren der Einheit war diese Frage zumeist einfach zu beantworten. Drei Jahrzehnte später funktionieren solche Zuordnungen immer weniger, NDR 2019, 3:43 Min.

Ossi or Wessi? – This question was generally easy to answer in the first years after reunification. Three decades later, such classifications tend to work less well, NDR 2019, 3:43 mins.

UM БИ
BRUCH UM
OST 18

Polska w strefie Schengen

SŁUBICE -
FRANKFURT (O)
20./21.12.2007

NACHBARN
NEIGHBOURS

Über die Brücke zwischen Frankfurt (Oder) und Słubice streben heute täglich einkaufslustige Deutsche nach Polen, wo Obst und Gemüse halb so teuer sind und doppelt so gut sein sollen. Aber auch Dienstleistungen vom Friseur bis zum Zahnarzt sind billig. Die Europa-Universität Viadrina und das Collegium Polonicum arbeiten gut zusammen. In der Nacht des 21. Dezember 2007, als die letzten Grenzsperren fallen, singen deutsche und polnische Studenten auf der Brücke gemeinsam die Europahymne. Heute muss man anscheinend nicht mehr beweisen, dass alle Menschen Brüder werden, wie es in der „Ode an die Freude" heißt. Kaum jemand erinnert sich mehr daran, dass wohl keine Grenze in Europa häufiger verschoben worden ist als diejenige zwischen Polen und Deutschen und dass jede dieser gewaltsamen Verschiebungen Not und Leid über die Menschen gebracht hat. Zum ersten Mal in der Geschichte lebt Deutschland mit allen Nachbarn in Frieden. Vielleicht ist es das Erfolgsrezept der deutschen Wiedervereinigung, dass sie sich als Teil der europäischen Vereinigung vollzogen hat.

To this day, German shoppers head to Poland every day across the bridge between Frankfurt an der Oder and Słubice, where fruit and vegetables are said to be half the price and twice as good. Services ranging from hairdressing to dentistry are cheaper too. The European University Viadrina and the Collegium Polonicum work well together. During the night of 21st December 2007, as the final border fortifications came down, German and Polish students sang the European anthem on the bridge. Today, it seems there is no longer any need to prove that we are all brothers and sisters as is stated in the "Ode to Joy". Barely anyone still remembers that no other border in Europe was moved as frequently as the one between Poland and Germany, and that each one of these violent shifts brought with it pain and suffering. For the first time in its history, Germany lives peacefully alongside all its neighbours. Perhaps the key to success of the reunification of Germany was that it happened to coincide with the unification of Europe.

18-01   Hunderte Menschen feiern am 21. Dezember 2007 kurz nach 0:00 Uhr am Grenzübergang Frankfurt (Oder) den Wegfall der Grenzkontrollen.
Shortly after midnight on 21st December 2007, hundreds of people celebrate the removal of border controls at the crossing in Frankfurt an der Oder.

18-02   Als am 8. April 1991 die Visumspflicht für polnische Bürger endet, attackieren deutsche Neonazis die ersten polnischen Besucher. Erst massive Polizeipräsenz kann einen sicheren Grenzverkehr gewährleisten.
German neo-Nazis attack the first Polish visitors after visa requirements for Polish citizens are lifted on 8th April 1991. Only a huge police presence guarantees safety at the border crossing.

18-03   Als „Friedensgrenze" wurde in der Propaganda bis 1989 die Grenze zwischen der DDR und Polen bezeichnet. 1992 ist dies der Name eines Cafés in deren Nähe.
The border between the GDR and Poland was referred to as the "Friedensgrenze" ("border of peace") in propaganda until 1989. In 1992, a nearby café takes this name.

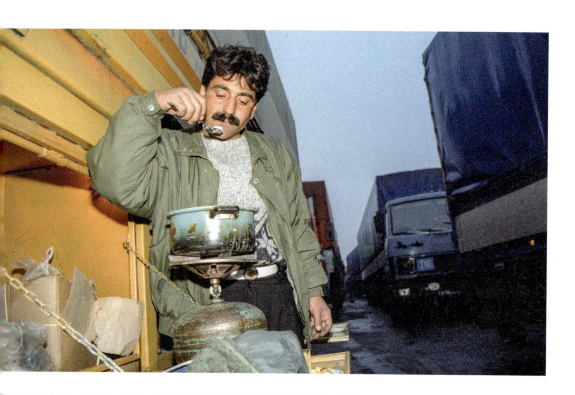

18-04   Auch weiterhin bleiben für Lkw-Fahrer kilometerlange Staus vor der Grenze und Wartezeiten von
mehreren Tagen Normalität. Foto: 1993.
*Kilometre-long traffic jams before the border and wait times of several days are normal for a long time.
Photo: 1993.*

18-05   In den 1990er Jahren blüht an der deutsch-polnischen Grenze der Schmuggel – nicht nur von
Zigaretten. Armutsprostitution gehört ebenso zum Alltag wie grenzüberschreitende Kriminalität.
Foto: 1993.
*In the 1990s, smuggling thrives at the German-Polish border – and it involves more than just cigarettes.
Poverty-induced prostitution is as much a part of everyday life as international criminal activity. Photo
1993.*

18-06   Die damit verbundenen Sorgen und Ängste tun dem Einkaufstourismus nach Polen jedoch keinen
Abbruch. Weihnachtseinkäufer auf dem „Polenmarkt" in Słubice im Dezember 1996.
*The associated concerns and fears do nothing to reduce the number of shopping tourism trips to Poland.
Christmas shoppers at the Polish market in Słubice in December 1996.*

18-07   Die polnisch-deutsche Universität Viadrina in Frankfurt (Oder), 1996.
The European University Viadrina in Frankfurt an der Oder, 1996.

VIDEO
Slubfurt: Wie Deutsche und Polen
zusammenwachsen, DW TV, 3:13 Min.

*Slubfurt: How Germans and Poles are
growing together, DW TV, 3:13 mins.*

VIDEO
Grenzenlos – Die Überwindung der kommunistischen Diktaturen Osteuropas ebnete den Weg zur europäischen Integration. Inner-europäische Grenzen sind jedoch mehr als Markierungen am Fahrbahnrand, NDR 2019, 2:15 Min.

Frictionless – The triumph over the communist dictatorship of Eastern Europe paved the way for European integration. Yet European borders are still more than just markings at the roadside, NDR 2019, 2:15 mins.

UM ꟽꟼ
BRUCH UM
OST '19

UNVOLLENDET
UNFINISHED

Bei vielen Ostdeutschen ist die Stimmung heute mies. Manche sagen, sie sei so mies wie 1989, als das Volk die SED-Führung zum Teufel jagte. Daran knüpft die rechtspopulistische AfD an. „Der Osten steht auf", oder „Vollende die Wende" heißt es auf den Wahlplakaten dieser Partei. Diese Stimmung steht in einem bemerkenswerten Widerspruch zur allgemeinen Entwicklung des Landes. Sicher: Nach wie vor sind im Osten die Gehälter, Vermögen und die Produktivität geringer und ist die Arbeitslosigkeit höher als im Westen. Aber im Vergleich zu den 1990er Jahren hat sich dort die Wirtschaftskraft verdoppelt, und die Arbeitslosenquote lag im August 2019 mit 6,4 Prozent zwei Drittel unter dem Stand von 2000. Vergleicht man hier Sachsen (5,4 %) und Thüringen (5,3 %) mit Bremen (10,3 %) oder auch Nordrhein-Westfalen (6,7 %), wird eines deutlich: Die soziale Kluft verläuft längst nicht mehr vorrangig zwischen Ost und West. Wer in das Klagelied vom abgehängten Osten einstimmt, der schürt nicht nur Unfrieden, sondern auch das Feuer jener, die darauf ihr populistisches Süppchen kochen.

Nowadays, the atmosphere among many former East Germans is miserable. Some say it is as miserable as in 1989 when the people sent the SED leadership packing. The populist right-wing AfD party is latching on to this. The party's election posters are emblazoned with "Der Osten steht auf" ('The East is rising up') and "Vollende die Wende" ('Finish the revolution'). This atmosphere starkly contradicts the country's overall development. For sure, assets are still less valuable, salaries and productivity still lower and unemployment still higher in former East Germany than the former West. But in comparison with the 1990s, the region's economic strength has doubled and, in August 2019, the unemployment rate was 6.4%: two thirds lower than the figure in the year 2000. Compare Saxony (5.4%) and Thuringia (5.3%) with Bremen (10.3%) or even North-Rhine Westphalia (6.7%), and one thing becomes clear – the predominant social divide is no longer between East and West. Those who join in with the lament of the left-behind East not only incite unrest but also stoke the flames of populism.

19-01   Irgendwo in Berlin, 2. Oktober 2015.
         Somewhere in Berlin, 2nd October 2015.

19-02   Eine Menschenkette soll am 13. Februar 2013, dem Jahrestag der Bombardierung Dresdens im Zweiten Weltkrieg, den Aufmarsch rechtsextremer Demonstranten in der Innenstadt verhindern.
         On 13th February 2013, the anniversary of the bombing of Dresden in the Second World War, a human chain aims to prevent a march by extreme right-wing demonstrators through the city centre.

19-03   „Wende 2.0 – Friedliche Revolution mit dem Stimmzettel". Im Landtagswahlkampf 2019 in Brandenburg und Sachsen setzt die AfD die Demokratie des vereinten Deutschlands mit der SED-Diktatur gleich.
         "Wende 2.0 – Peaceful Revolution with the ballot paper". In the 2019 state election campaigns in Brandenburg and Saxony, the AfD equates the democracy of reunified Germany with the SED dictatorship.

19-04   Nach dem gescheiterten Versuch in die Synagoge in Halle (Saale) einzudringen, um die dort versammelten Gläubigen zu töten, erschießt ein Rechtsextremist am 9. Oktober 2019 eine Passantin sowie den Gast eines Schnellimbisses. Vier Tage später legt dessen Inhaber bei einer Gedenkveranstaltung ein Blumengebinde nieder.
After a failed attempt to infiltrate the synagogue in Halle (Saale) in order to kill the worshippers gathered there, a right-wing extremist shoots dead a passer-by and a diner at a fast food restaurant on 9th October 2019. Four days later, the restaurant's owner lays a bundle of flowers at a memorial service.

19-05   Eine Straße in Gelsenkirchen (Nordrhein-Westfalen) im April 2017. Die Ruhrgebietsstadt hat eine Arbeitslosenquote von 14 Prozent.
A street in Gelsenkirchen (North-Rhine Westphalia) in April 2017. The Ruhr city has an unemployment rate of 14%.

19-06   Der Marktplatz in Güstrow (Mecklenburg-Vorpommern), 2019.
The market square in Güstrow (Mecklenburg-Western Pomerania), 2019.

19-07   „Azubis gesucht" steht auf einem Banner an einer Baustelle in Ahlbeck (Mecklenburg-Vorpommern).
A banner on a building site in Ahlbeck (Mecklenburg-Western Pomerania) declares "apprentices wanted".

VIDEO
3te Generation Ostdeutschland auf Tour und vor Ort,
LpB Brandenburg / Youtube, 3:26 Min.

*3te Generation Ostdeutschland initiative on tour and on
the ground, LpB Brandenburg / YouTube, 3:26 mins.*

VIDEO

Unverständnis – statt Verständigung. Die Folgen von Kränkungen sind langlebig, Vorurteile hartnäckig. Sie treffen auch Menschen, die 1989 und später geboren wurden ..., NDR 2019, 4:30 Min.

Incomprehension instead of understanding. The consequences of insults are long-lasting and prejudices are stubborn. They also affect people who were born in 1989 and later ..., NDR 2019, 4:30 mins.

UM WO UM
BRUCH
OST 20

ZWISCHENFAZIT
INTERIM CONCLUSION

Die Erinnerung an die Jahre des Umbruchs Ost stand lange im Schatten der turbulenten und bildmächtigen Monate zwischen der Friedlichen Revolution im Herbst 1989 und der Wiedervereinigung am 3. Oktober 1990. Erst in jüngerer Zeit machen Fernsehdokumentationen, Spielfilme, Romane, aber auch Museen die Geschichte des vereinten Deutschlands verstärkt zum Thema. Tatsächlich bieten die Jahre seit der Wiedervereinigung viel Stoff zum Nachdenken und Nachfragen: Wie geht man angemessen mit totalitären Vergangenheiten um? Wie sind kollektive Traumatisierungen zu vermeiden, wie soziale und wirtschaftliche Ungleichheiten innerhalb eines Landes zu überwinden? Und dies alles in einer Welt, die sich rasant wandelt. Der Schriftsteller Stefan Heym hat die DDR als eine „Fußnote der Geschichte" bezeichnet. Doch wer die Geschichte der deutschen Einheit mit all ihren Versäumnissen und Erfolgen verstehen will, der darf die Folgen von SED-Diktatur und deutscher Teilung nicht aus dem Blick verlieren.

Recollections of the year of transformation in the East were overshadowed for a long time by the turbulent and visually powerful months between the Peaceful Revolution in the autumn of 1989 and the reunification on 3rd October 1990. Only recently have television documentaries, feature films, novels and museums begun to focus more intently on the history of reunified Germany. Indeed, the years since the reunification offer plenty of material for thought and consideration. What is the appropriate way to approach a totalitarian past? How can collective trauma be avoided, and how can social and financial inequalities inside a country be overcome? And all of this in a world that is constantly changing. The author Stefan Heym described the GDR as a "footnote in history". However, anybody who wishes to understand the history of German reunification with all its successes and failures must not lose sight of the consequences of the SED dictatorship and the partition of Germany.

VIDEO
Alles eins? – Menschen verschiedener Generationen blicken sehr unterschiedlich auf den Umbruch von Lebenswelten. Sie ziehen Bilanz. Vorläufig, NDR 2019, 3:10 Min.

All united? – People from different generations perceive the breakup of ways of life very differently. They balance each other out. Provisional, NDR 2019, 3:10 mins.

20-01 Seit 1998 ist das Trabi-Storchennest der Mühle Bechlin an der B 167 vor Neuruppin Wahrzeichen und Touristenattraktion.
The Trabi-Storchennest (lit. "Trabi stork's nest") at the Bechlin Mill next to the B 167 outside Neuruppin has been a landmark and tourist attraction since 1998.

FOTO / *PHOTO:*

02-01	Harald Hauswald / Ostkreuz / Bundesstiftung Aufarbeitung
02-02	Ann-Christine Jansson / Bundesstiftung Aufarbeitung
02-03	Daniel Biskup / Bundesstiftung Aufarbeitung
02-04	picture alliance / dpa / Dieter Roosen
02-05	Yorck Maecke / GAFF / laif
02-06	picture alliance / dpa / Michael Jung
02-07	picture alliance / ZB / Paul Glaser
03-01	Halle (Saale), 1991; Daniel Biskup / Bundesstiftung Aufarbeitung
03-02	Harald Hauswald / Ostkreuz / Bundesstiftung Aufarbeitung
03-03	Daniel Biskup / Bundesstiftung Aufarbeitung
03-04	Ann-Christine Jansson / Bundesstiftung Aufarbeitung
03-05	Harald Hauswald / Ostkreuz / Bundesstiftung Aufarbeitung
03-06	Harald Hauswald / Ostkreuz / Bundesstiftung Aufarbeitung
03-07	Ann-Christine Jansson / Bundesstiftung Aufarbeitung
04-01	Ann-Christine Jansson / Bundesstiftung Aufarbeitung
04-02	Daniel Biskup / Bundesstiftung Aufarbeitung
04-03	Daniel Biskup / Bundesstiftung Aufarbeitung
04-04	Ann-Christine Jansson / Bundesstiftung Aufarbeitung
04-05	Ann-Christine Jansson / Bundesstiftung Aufarbeitung
04-06	picture alliance / ZB / Matthias Hiekel
04-07	Nicole Maskus / laif
05-01	Wolfgang Volz / laif
05-02	picture alliance / dpa / Andreas Altwein
05-03	General-Anzeiger Bonn / Jürgen Pätow
05-04	picture alliance / dpa / Frank Kleefeldt
05-05	picture alliance / dpa / ZB / Ralf Hirschberger
05-06	picture alliance / ZB / Rainer Weisflog
05-07	Ann-Christine Jansson / Bundesstiftung Aufarbeitung
06-01	picture alliance / ZB / Wolfgang Thieme
06-02	picture alliance / Matthias Hiekel
06-03	picture alliance / ZB / Heinz Hirndorf
06-04	Harald Hauswald / Ostkreuz / Bundesstiftung Aufarbeitung
06-05	Daniel Biskup / Bundesstiftung Aufarbeitung
06-06	picture alliance
06-07	picture alliance / ZB / Waltraud Grubitzsch
07-01	picture alliance / ZB / Bernd Settnik
07-02	Harald Hauswald / Ostkreuz / Bundesstiftung Aufarbeitung
07-03	Ann-Christine Jansson / Bundesstiftung Aufarbeitung
07-04	picture alliance / ZB / Hannes Müller
07-05	Harald Hauswald / Ostkreuz / Bundesstiftung Aufarbeitung
07-06	picture alliance / ZB / Wolfgang Kumm
07-07	picture alliance / ZB / Bernd Wüstneck
08-01	Rolf Nobel / VISUM
08-02	Ann-Christine Jansson / Bundesstiftung Aufarbeitung
08-03	Daniel Biskup / Bundesstiftung Aufarbeitung
08-04	Stefan Boness / IPON
08-05	Daniel Biskup / Bundesstiftung Aufarbeitung
08-06	picture alliance / ZB / Hendrik Schmidt
08-07	picture alliance / ZB / Patrick Pleul
09-01	Ann-Christine Jansson / Bundesstiftung Aufarbeitung
09-02	Ann-Christine Jansson / Bundesstiftung Aufarbeitung
09-03	Ann-Christine Jansson / Bundesstiftung Aufarbeitung
09-04	picture alliance / ZB / Paul Glaser
09-05	Ann-Christine Jansson / Bundesstiftung Aufarbeitung
09-06	Daniel Biskup / Bundesstiftung Aufarbeitung
09-07	Ann-Christine Jansson / Bundesstiftung Aufarbeitung
10-01	picture alliance / ZB / Paul Glaser
10-02	picture alliance / ZB / Ralf Hirschberger
10-03	picture alliance / ZB / Jan-Peter Kasper
10-04	picture alliance / dpa / Hartmut Reeh
10-05	picture alliance / ZB / Heinz Hirndorf
10-06	picture alliance / ZB / Paul Glaser
10-07	picture alliance / ZB / Paul Glaser

11-01	Daniel Biskup / Bundesstiftung Aufarbeitung
11-02	Ann-Christine Jansson / Bundesstiftung Aufarbeitung
11-03	Daniel Biskup / Bundesstiftung Aufarbeitung
11-04	Ann-Christine Jansson / Bundesstiftung Aufarbeitung
11-05	Daniel Biskup / Bundesstiftung Aufarbeitung
11-06	picture alliance / ZB / Helmut Schaar
11-07	picture alliance / ZB / Peer Grimm
12-01	picture alliance / ZB / Peter Förster
12-02	Harald Hauswald / Ostkreuz / Bundesstiftung Aufarbeitung
12-03	Jordis Antonia Schlösser / Ostkreuz
12-04	picture alliance / ZB / Reinhard Kaufhold
12-05	Harald Hauswald / Ostkreuz / Bundesstiftung Aufarbeitung
12-06	picture alliance / ZB / Wolfgang Thieme
12-07	Daniel Biskup / Bundesstiftung Aufarbeitung
13-01	picture alliance / dpa / Rainer Jensen
13-02	Daniel Biskup / Bundesstiftung Aufarbeitung
13-03	picture alliance / ZB / Martin Förster
13-04	Harald Hauswald / Ostkreuz / Bundesstiftung Aufarbeitung
13-05	picture alliance / ZB / Heinz Hirndorf
13-06	picture alliance / dpa / Tim Brakemeier
13-07	picture alliance / dpa-Zentralbild / Jens Büttner
14-01	picture alliance / dpa-Zentralbild / Peer Grimm
14-02	picture alliance / ZB / Paul Glaser
14-03	picture alliance / ZB / Jens Kalaene
14-04	picture alliance / ZB / ddrbildarchiv / Lange
14-05	Ann-Christine Jansson / Bundesstiftung Aufarbeitung
14-06	Ann-Christine Jansson / Bundesstiftung Aufarbeitung
14-07	picture alliance / ZB / Stefan Sauer
15-01	Sibylle Bergemann / Ostkreuz
15-02	Harald Hauswald / Ostkreuz / Bundesstiftung Aufarbeitung
15-03	picture alliance / dpa / Rainer Weisflog
15-04	Ann-Christine Jansson / Bundesstiftung Aufarbeitung
15-05	Daniel Biskup / Bundesstiftung Aufarbeitung
15-06	Harald Hauswald / Ostkreuz / Bundesstiftung Aufarbeitung
15-07	Daniel Biskup / Bundesstiftung Aufarbeitung
16-01	Daniel Biskup / Bundesstiftung Aufarbeitung
16-02	picture alliance / ZB / Ralf Hirschberger
16-03	picture alliance / ZB / Peter Förster
16-04	Ann-Christine Jansson / Bundesstiftung Aufarbeitung
16-05	Ann-Christine Jansson / Bundesstiftung Aufarbeitung
16-06	Ann-Christine Jansson / Bundesstiftung Aufarbeitung
16-07	picture alliance / ZB / Jens Büttner
17-01	SZ Photo / Jochen Eckel
17-02	picture alliance / ZB / euroluftbild.de / Lothar Willmann
17-03	picture alliance
17-04	picture alliance / dpa / Armin Weigel
17-05	picture alliance / ZB / Ralf Hirschberger
17-06	picture alliance / ZB / Jens Kalaene
17-07	picture alliance / ZB / Rudolf Bonß
18-01	picture alliance / dpa / Patrick Pleul
18-02	Ann-Christine Jansson / Bundesstiftung Aufarbeitung
18-03	Ann-Christine Jansson / Bundesstiftung Aufarbeitung
18-04	Ann-Christine Jansson / Bundesstiftung Aufarbeitung
18-05	Ann-Christine Jansson / Bundesstiftung Aufarbeitung
18-06	picture alliance / dpa / ZB / Jens Kalaene
18-07	picture alliance / ZB / Hubert Link
19-01	picture alliance / dpa / Rainer Jensen
19-02	picture alliance / dpa-Zentralbild / Arno Burgi
19-03	Königs Wusterhausen; Fritz Engel / laif
19-04	picture alliance / dpa-Zentralbild / Hendrik Schmidt
19-05	picture alliance / Jochen Eckel
19-06	Daniel Biskup / Bundesstiftung Aufarbeitung
19-07	picture alliance / dpa-Zentralbild / Jens Kalaene
20-01	picture alliance / dpa-Zentralbild / Jens Büttner